Tell Your Story

The story of one woman's struggle with a rare form of cancer, its triumphs and its setbacks, simply and dramatically told.

Susan Overton-Smith

Blessings dear Andy and Ian,

Sue Overton-Smith.

ISBN: 978-1-7398006-0-4

Cover picture taken from a watercolour by the author at an Art Class in a Shipley garden in 2001.

In memory of Colin Urquhart whose words inspired me

and

To my husband Roger, and our sons Nicholas and James, who lived through this with me.

ACKNOWLEDGMENTS

To all those who have encouraged me, and helped me with the production of this book, those who prayed for me, and all those who treated me in hospital and helped save my life, together with all who cared for and looked after me then and since, for you I shall always be thankful. As I hope this book shows, you have been such an important part of my life and have never been forgotten.

CONTENTS

PREFACE

Writing a book is the last thing I thought I would ever do. I found the whole experience so traumatic that when people suggested this to me twenty years ago I couldn't even contemplate it. I wanted to forget and in some ways I still do, although I can at last cope with the memories to a certain extent. Reliving those memories was possibly the reason why I began to feel somewhat depressed. I am normally optimistic and cheerful, wanting to look ahead but this process has forced me to be introspective which has not always been helpful. Some people would argue that it has helped me to come to terms with it and perhaps that is true; I don't know.

I now feel a compelling urge to tell my story because I hope that by so doing, I shall help promote further understanding of someone who finds him or herself in a similar situation.

There have been so many changes: independence to dependence, being in control to being controlled, being surrounded by children to being with adults or even alone, using my voice most of the time to enforced silence, preparing plans and following them to not knowing what will happen next, taking certain things for granted such as holidays, eating, drinking, talking and singing to valuing them beyond measure and being full of vitality to extreme tiredness BUT there is a positive side. When one has a potentially life-threatening illness, one receives love from so many people. It helps to make everything more bearable. I have met all kinds of new and interesting people. I've had time to develop my interest in painting and there has been the opportunity to grow spiritually. It has allowed time for saying those things we should say to one another but so often leave unsaid.

With my illness my life changed suddenly, without warning. I am so grateful for the Lord's grace and mercy as He took me through this. He had allowed me to go to Jerusalem first, on Easter Day 1999, and to be greatly affected at the Garden of Gethsemane. We went into the Church of the Nations where inside was a plaque which had a verse from the gospel of Luke, describing Jesus' agony the night before He died:

'And being in agony, He prayed more earnestly. Then His sweat became like great drops of blood falling down to the ground.' He endured the pain and humiliation of the cross in our stead because He loved us so much.

This experience came to mind many times whilst I was in hospital and gave me the strength to face the situation. Whatever I was going through I was surrounded by love and support, whereas Jesus endured far worse pain than I had to and was surrounded by hatred.

* * * * *

At first, I was impatient to get better but gradually, over the first year and a half since the main operation, I had learned to be patient. For the first year, people said I was progressing in leaps and bounds. This was deeply encouraging and in July 2001 there was a marked improvement. The swelling had gone down noticeably on one side of my tongue which helped me to speak a little better but then the progress became more gradual. I seemed to have reached a plateau which was not quite level - the gradient was slight. It was moving ever so slowly in an upward direction.

I had to admit to feelings of frustration, especially as far as my inability to swallow was concerned. I knew both my surgeon and my speech therapist found the long wait difficult and I remember feeling that I was letting my surgeon down by not performing in the right way. It led to a lot of soul searching. Was I really not trying hard enough? I was attempting to swallow several times a day. I felt so much pressure to try harder. I thought I merely had to be patient and that when the swelling of the tongue eventually went down and the nerves regenerated themselves the tongue would become more mobile again. Then I would regain my clarity of speech and be able to swallow all at the same time. Medical evidence concerning tracheostomies and gastro-nasal tubes suggested that my optimism was not valid.

I still have faith today that it will happen. I am looking forward to being normal again. Eating and drinking, in a social context, form such an important bonding process between people that, not only do I feel left out, I am also being distanced from those around me with every mouthful they share together. I want them to relax but I have noticed that other people themselves feel deeply uncomfortable about having to eat or drink in my presence. It is such a deep instinct within us all, subconsciously, to bond with others by offering food or drink that many people still find themselves offering it to me even though they already know that I cannot accept. I get over it by looking closely at the food and savouring the wonderful smells.

In the privacy of my own home and with some of our best friends I can feel more included by sampling whatever is on offer. Unfortunately, it means I have to excuse myself from the table several times during the meal, which is embarrassing and not good etiquette, so that is why I have to know people well. As well as enabling me to enjoy the pleasure of tasting and experiencing the sensation of chewing, this helps me to partake in the bonding process. The disadvantage is that I miss out on a large part of the conversation.

I still find it immensely difficult when everyone around me is having a special meal. Everything looks and smells so good whereas I am merely having my hunger assuaged via my feeding machine so that I am hardly aware that I am eating. I have grown more used to missing normal meals on a daily basis, so much so that there are occasions when it comes to bedtime and I have completely forgotten to fix up my feed during the evening. There are times when the machine feels extra heavy and cumbersome, especially when I am moving about in the kitchen. It is like being a dog on a lead or a donkey tethered with a rope. If I put the machine down, I can wander just so far before it pulls me up tight, yanking hard at the PEG site where the tube enters the stomach. This also occurs when the tube gets caught around a knob on one of the drawers or doors. As well as causing pain, I have worried that the stoma button might be pulled out. I know that this wonderful machine is keeping me alive so I do not wish to complain but I long for the day when I am independent of it.

In the meantime, I must make the best of my situation and be thankful that it enables me to live as full a life as I do. If it makes other people thankful for things they have previously taken for granted then that's a positive thing to have come out of it.

1: JULY 1999

"I shall be honest with you and tell you the good news or the bad news, whichever it turns out to be." Mr. McPherson looked me in the eye and the seriousness of the situation began to sink in yet it still seemed unreal.

Only the week before I had been celebrating the end of term, enjoying a barbecue lunch with friends and listening to a jazz band playing in the garden of a local pub. Sitting in the sunshine I seemingly hadn't a care in the world yet within days my life would be turned upside down. The future suddenly seemed uncertain.

* * * * *

It all began innocently enough, with a sore throat. Everyone around me had one; I was a teacher. It was par for the course, especially in the Summer Term. Not that I needed to raise my voice particularly but a voice was essential in my occupation. Still, it didn't seem unusual. However, there was something that did concern me. I was finding it difficult to swallow. It felt as though the muscles in my tongue weren't working properly. It was taking a long time to eat meals. Whenever I was on playground duty, and also having to prepare for the afternoon's lessons, time for eating was limited so every minute was precious. I could easily eat lunch in ten minutes if I had to, but it had become harder to reach my target and at the end of term lunch I had been last to finish. "You can always tell who's been talking," someone teased. I smiled and the chatter around me continued as I made an effort to finish my meal. The end of term lunch was a wonderful way to unwind, and we were happy. Exhausted after the hectic Summer Term, everyone was looking forward to being able to relax at last.

My husband, Roger, and I were due to go with our son and his family to a favourite haunt of ours in Cornwall, around the time of the Eclipse, but our holiday plans were now having to be put on hold.

At the weekend a friend and colleague suggested that my husband and I might like to join her family and another friend for a barbecue lunch at a local pub where there was to be a jazz band playing in the garden. It sounded a delightful idea so we were only too pleased to join them.

The sun was shining and there was plenty of cheerful chatter as we ordered delicious items from the menu, the relaxing melodies of the jazz band wafting through the air together with the mouthwatering smells emanating from the barbecue. When the food arrived, I apologised to my friend's mother for taking so long to eat my meal. Explaining that I was finding it difficult to swallow, she responded immediately by advising me to go to the doctor.

I had hoped that my difficulty in swallowing would disappear with rest but this hadn't happened so, having been prompted by her advice, I went to the Open Surgery on Saturday 24th July 1999 immediately after my appointment with the dentist. It didn't occur to me to mention my problem to the dentist but at least my teeth were in good order so, after a scale and polish, I walked in the sunshine, feeling concerned but not unduly worried, to the doctor's surgery. Once there I awaited my turn, chatting to the man sitting next to me who happened to be doing a crossword. We had fun thinking of the answers together. Now I heard my name being called.

Dr Peter Hard listened carefully as I told him of my problem. He examined my mouth and throat but there was nothing to be seen. Suspecting something serious, he said that he was going to refer me to a specialist at St Richard's Hospital in Chichester and I would hear when I had an appointment.

I was somewhat surprised by this turn of events as I'd expected the solution to be straightforward and that I'd be back to normal again in a few days. Once we were at home I continued to look in the mirror at my tongue and throat but their appearance didn't fit with the way they felt.

Life continued as normal but the following afternoon, when I looked in the mirror, I was able to see something at last but the size of it both shocked and surprised me. I called my husband,

"Roger, come and look at this. There's a patch on my throat." Roger stared in disbelief,

"That isn't in your throat. It's your tongue!"

A fairly large pale yellow lump had appeared at the back of my tongue. My first reaction was that it was full of pus and was the reason that I'd had so much difficulty in swallowing. I thought that perhaps my tongue had been pierced by something sharp like a fish bone and had subsequently become infected. As it was a Sunday I telephoned the Surgery first thing on the Monday morning, 26th July. Dr. Hard asked me to come straight away and he'd look at it. Like me, he was amazed at the size of the lump and couldn't believe he hadn't seen it on the Saturday, but neither had I. It can't have been obvious then because the dentist would have noticed it.

I don't think the mind always faces up to anything too terrible straight away; it sometimes needs time to adjust, automatically looking for an innocent explanation. Surely the doctor would now lance it and give me antibiotics to disperse it and I would feel well again in a few days. My innocence was to be short lived.

At least we now had evidence relating to the problem. However, instead of the expected antibiotics and possible draining of the site, Dr Hard said that he now knew which specialist I should see. He gave us his home telephone number so that we could let him know what the specialist had said.

Being of an inquisitive nature and always interested in medical matters, I went to the library on that Monday morning and poured over the relevant medical books, concentrating on the 'tongue' section, coming to the conclusion that this 'lump of pus' on my tongue was most probably a tumour of some kind. I didn't smoke or drink, except for the occasional glass of wine, which seem to be the most common reasons for tumours in this region. At least I was aware of the potential gravity of my illness so I wasn't surprised when David MacPherson, the Consultant Surgeon, said to me next day, Tuesday 27th July, that he would be honest with me and tell me the good news or the bad news, whichever it might turn out to be. After listening to my account of the symptoms he asked me to come through to be examined. I was about to have my first experience of a nasendoscopy. A long, narrow black tube with a camera and light at the end was passed up one nostril and on down the throat so that Mr. MacPherson could see what was happening at the back of my tongue. Although an anaesthetic spray had been used beforehand, I felt slight discomfort and did not particularly enjoy the experience. As I had hay fever there was a lot of congestion which can't have helped. After some consideration, I was booked in to have a biopsy the following Tuesday 3rd August and was to expect an overnight stay in hospital.

I felt increasingly lethargic during that week and spent most of my time lying on the bed not even feeling like reading which I normally enjoy. As the days passed by, the lump seemed to increase in size and I could eat less and less. My husband was worried because my mother had died, years before, of cancer which had first presented itself as a lump on her neck and a very sore throat. Events did not treat her kindly and the rapid changes happening to me over these few days, between seeing the specialist and having the biopsy, caused my husband to ring my GP to voice his concern.

My GP phoned the hospital hoping to speak to David MacPherson but he'd just left. A fellow consultant, Mr. Townend, obligingly said he'd have a look at my throat that day, after his clinic at Goring Hall, and he'd probably be able to put our minds at rest as he would be able to tell, at a glance, whether the growth were malignant or benign.

I felt somewhat nervous as I drove along to meet him because I would soon know, one way or the other, the nature of this lump. Once I'd arrived, I sat on a chair in the comfortable waiting room turning the pages of a magazine, seeing but unseeing, not fully comprehending the words in front of me. I did not have to wait long. Mr. Townend cheerfully came to greet me and ushered me into his room. We spoke for a few minutes and then I lay on a couch while he shone a light into my mouth and took as good a look as he could in the circumstances. Unfortunately, my mind was not put at rest. He had seemed so buoyant when he'd greeted me but his manner had become grave as he informed me that it was definitely a growth of some kind but that he could not tell which sort it was. He said that it needed examining more closely and only a biopsy would tell.

I remember walking back to my car, in the afternoon sunshine, feeling stunned. Somehow I knew what the prognosis would be. Mr. Townend must suspect it to be cancerous. It had been very kind of him to look. At least I was gradually becoming prepared for the eventual outcome.

Roger and I had been looking forward to going to a 'Salmon and Strawberry Supper' on the Friday evening, in aid of CHASE, a charity raising money to build a children's hospice on the Loseley Estate at Godalming, Surrey. Several of our friends from church were there and no sooner had we arrived than some of them were asking for the latest bulletin. We chatted for a while before moving onto the terrace where groups of people were mingling with their drinks before the meal. As we stepped out there, from the house, a dear friend, Bob, asked what we'd like to drink. At first I said I'd just have water but he insisted that I have something more than that. Of course, not knowing the situation, he misconstrued my hesitation and teased me. Normally I would have laughed at his harmless banter but, on this occasion, I could feel the tears were very close so I accepted my orange as graciously as I could and rather shakily turned back to his wife, Jenny, who understood and said she'd explain the situation to Bob later.

I asked for very small portions of food although it looked and smelled delicious. Our new rector was aware of my plight and sat with me. An old friend from schooldays joined us and others soon gathered around the table. The conversation was interesting but I had to send my plate back almost untouched. It had been too difficult to swallow the food and the orange hurt my throat. I managed to eat the soft mousse of the dessert but had been given only a small portion as I had left so much of the first course. Daphne is a superb cook and I was feeling acutely embarrassed as I felt it must have hurt her feelings. It was most frustrating not being able to eat all this beautiful food. Every time I swallowed it was an effort, and my throat gave a peculiar gurgling sound.

The following day, we were due to meet an old University friend, Graham, and his wife, Jane, for a picnic in the grounds of Chichester Festival Theatre, before the matinee. It was wonderful to see them again. Knowing that I could no longer eat normal food, I took some soft tinned asparagus to be followed by mashed banana and raspberries accompanied by a few sips of water. It was again most frustrating having to sit there while the others had an exciting looking dip with their chilled wine followed by all manner of delicious foods. My speech was also affected by this stage so I had to leave most of the talking to the other three. Although everyone had been friendly and we had thoroughly enjoyed our friends' company, this was the beginning of my first taste of feeling an outsider.

The play we had come to see that afternoon was 'Barnum', featuring Peter Duncan of 'Blue Peter' fame. The part which stands out in my memory is when he had to walk on a tightrope fairly high above the stage. I was amazed that he should have to do that as part of his acting, but he survived with flying colours. It was most enjoyable.

I tried to suck a throat sweet during the performance but this proved difficult as it produced extra saliva which meant that, every time I swallowed, I was, yet again, making embarrassing gurgling sounds. I was anxious not to distract the people around me from the play, so I had to hold the saliva in my mouth and choose my moments carefully.

After bidding farewell to our friends, we drove home via my cousin's house as she was having a barbecue to which we'd been invited. It was a warm summer's evening. Friends and family were seated around the swimming pool. We donned costumes and slid into the warm water. A couple of others joined us. It was bliss. The state of my throat was irrelevant here; we were all on equal terms. After swimming a few lengths, we had fun playing with the various pool accessories - diving, racing and splashing one another in a friendly way. Eventually we climbed out, dripping, wrapped ourselves in our towels and went inside to shower and change. It had been so relaxing in the water and now we were tingling from the welcome exertion of exercise.

Roger was given a plate piled high with barbecued meat and diverse salads. I surveyed the food on the table for something I could manage. I tried a raspberry. I had always loved fruit, especially raspberries, but the acid hurt my throat. It was no good. I could not eat. I sipped some water but couldn't seem to swallow until my cousin, Jan, took me along to her new American refrigerator which dispensed ice cold water at the touch of a button. I was able to drink at last. It was wonderful. I was very thirsty. Using a straw, I managed to drink four whole glasses of iced water that evening.

That was the last time I was able to drink properly before the biopsy on the Tuesday. From the Saturday evening onwards, I could no longer eat and could only sip water. I could feel my throat closing up and began to worry that I might not be able to breathe much longer.

2: FIRST BIOPSY

I don't remember much about the time between Saturday 31st July and going into hospital. I packed my bag for an overnight stay in St. Richard's, Chichester, where Mr. MacPherson was to perform the biopsy. I had now become drained of energy and just didn't know what to do with myself. Tuesday 3rd August couldn't come soon enough.

On arrival at the hospital, I was given a room of my own. Though sparsely furnished, it had cheerful curtains which contrasted with the dull greyness outside. Raindrops covered the windowpane as Roger and I watched the passing cars below. A nurse came to take my details. Her friendliness helped put us at ease. She helped me change into a hospital gown, a garment tied with tapes at the back, and which had 'Property of St.

Richard's Hospital' stamped all over it in tiny, colourful letters. The inferred message was that the patients weren't to be trusted not to steal hospital property. "No chance of that!" I thought.

"What are those?" I asked, looking in surprise at what the nurse was holding.

"These are anti-embolism stockings, to prevent a thrombosis in your legs. I'll show you the best way to put them on," she replied. Roger stayed with me for a while, but I recall little of what happened thereafter until I was wheeled into the ante-room prior to the operation.

I had never had one before, so everything was new to me. People seemed friendly. The assistant anaesthetist repeatedly flicked at the vein in the back of my left hand to make it prominent. It became extremely tender, so I was glad when he inserted the needle. He also put in a second one.

I was introduced to Doctor Kendall, the anaesthetist who would care for me during the operation. I explained to him my fear that I might wake up during the operation and feel everything but be completely unable to let anyone know, but he assured me that that would not happen. I began to relax and closed my eyes. The next thing I knew a nurse was waking me up. The biopsy hadn't taken long. I was surprised that it was all over and that I was awake again so quickly.

I have a vague recollection of being wheeled into a room on the intensive care ward. The nurse assigned to me was gentle and attentive. I wasn't really in pain, just slightly uncomfortable. The painkillers were mostly effective.

A long tube to humidify the oxygen stretched across my throat, joining another one in the middle which entered my trachea. The tube gurgled which bothered me. I felt panicky. I was finding it quite hard to breathe in much air. I tried to calm down. Finding myself unable to speak, I motioned to the nurse that I needed to write, whereupon she kindly gave me paper and a pen.

Mr. MacPherson came to explain what he had done. He apologised because I wouldn't be going home as originally planned. He told me that the lump had grown so big that the anaesthetist hadn't been able to push the tube down my airway so that, although it hadn't been discussed with me beforehand, it was imperative that I should have a tracheostomy.

I was full of questions. For how long would I have to have the tracheostomy? How long would the blocking and suctioning go on for? Had he cut just part of the lump away? I seemed to have a constant tickle in my chest. Was this normal?

Mr. MacPherson was both patient and

understanding. "I've taken some pieces of the lump for examination, and I've shaved some of it off so that you don't feel so uncomfortable when swallowing." I wanted to know all the facts, if possible. "The lump has grown very quickly and is most probably cancerous," he informed me. He went on to say that if the lump should be malignant, radio therapy plus possible surgery would be a better option than surgery alone. The latter would have to be invasive to be sure of removing all the cancer cells, which would mean losing my voice box, most of my tongue and therefore swallowing and control of my airway.

I was able to cope with the news about my tongue and airway but when Mr. MacPherson mentioned that I could ultimately lose my voice, I could not hold back the tears. My voice was precious to me. I had enjoyed reading stories to the children at school and had been looking forward to reading to my little grandson, William, and talking to him. I also loved singing. At both my schools my music teachers had each encouraged me to consider a career in it. The thought of no longer being able to speak or to sing overwhelmed me with an immense sense of loss. It can't be easy for surgeons when they have to break such news to their patients.

"Whilst survival is paramount," stressed Mr. MacPherson, "your quality of life has to be given the utmost consideration."

I was quickly coming to terms with remaining in hospital. Somehow, I felt vindicated. The alacrity with which the lump had grown seemed to have astounded everyone. Perhaps they now understood why I'd been frightened that soon I might not have been able to breathe. I wasn't therefore, particularly surprised by the turn of events. Had nature taken its course, I couldn't have survived. I knew that this operation had prolonged my life and I was grateful.

3: INTENSIVE CARE

Whilst lying in Intensive Care, I reflected on all those images I'd seen, in the News, of hospitals in war-stricken Sarajevo and considered how fortunate we are, in this country, to have our freedom and to have such high tech. equipment and good conditions for such an operation as mine to take place. Both there and here, however, I recognised the enormous dedication of the doctors and nurses. There was so much for which to be thankful.

There was a tube up my nose giving me liquid feed and another into my arm for a saline drip. Various drugs were administered via one tube or another at regular intervals. Wires connected me to a monitor which showed my heart rate, and my blood pressure was checked automatically. The apparatus around me emitted all sorts of electrical noises. Beeps and alarms frequently disturbed my sleep but were important for giving the medical staff vital information.

Since I'd had an opening made into my trachea, I had to be constantly nebulised to keep the airway moist. Every so often I would feel my throat tickle and give an involuntary cough, bringing up secretions from my lungs. Whenever this occurred, I had to be suctioned. A nurse would disconnect the large tube which stretched across me from the tracheostomy tube where it projected slightly from my throat. A long, narrow plastic tube would then be fed directly into my tracheostomy tube until I had a compelling urge to cough. The secretions from my lungs were then sucked up into the narrow tube to clear my airway. The discomfort made me dislike this process, but it was necessary to make breathing easier. The slight jolt of having the humidifying tube reattached invariably made my throat feel very tender even though the nurses tried their best to be gentle.

Having been deprived of nourishment during those last few days at home, the liquid feed soon made me feel better. I was constantly worried, however, in case I wouldn't be able to ask for a bedpan in time as I didn't have much warning. One soon loses one's dignity in hospital. It is most humbling. Every time the sheets were changed, I had to be rolled over on to my side. This usually made the long tube pull on my tracheostomy site, causing discomfort, so this became another procedure which I dreaded.

The beds, donated to the intensive care unit by Marks and Spencer, were wonderful. It was possible to adjust their position with very little effort. The mattresses themselves moved about gently, thus relieving unwanted pressure on our inert bodies. This was something I profoundly appreciated. Having a tracheostomy meant that I could no longer lie flat but had to have the upper part of my body at an angle of at least forty-five degrees to the base of the bed. It took a while to get used to sleeping in this position and not being able to turn over because of the humidifier and other tubes restricting my movements.

I was soon introduced to a physiotherapist, Nicky, who, apart from listening to my chest and suctioning me, gave me exercises to do with my legs and feet whilst also encouraging me to take occasional deep breaths. Feeling helpless in so many ways, I was glad to have something positive to do to aid my recovery.

4: VISITORS TO ITU

Visitors to the intensive care unit had to put on a plastic apron at the door to prevent the spread of infection. It was thus attired that Roger and our elder son, Nicholas, came to see me. They also washed their hands as an added precaution.

Just as I had been, Nicholas, too, had been anxious to know more. He had searched through medical books and used the internet to find out as much information as he could. At every stage he had tried to convince himself, and us, that my growth would fall into the benign category so I know that it must have been a shock when everything began to point in a less favourable direction. Nicholas had wanted to be a surgeon, from the age of six until he was sixteen, but had changed his mind to follow in his father's footsteps. Yet, from his reactions, his keen interest in every aspect of my illness and fascination for the machines around me, I am sure he would have been a suitable candidate. He certainly has the right temperament for it.

Faced with the seriousness of the situation, our minds were focused on the important things. It was an opportunity to express our feelings for one another and to give one another comfort and encouragement. I had written a message for Nicholas asking him to look after his father and make sure he didn't worry too much. I had asked both Nicholas and Roger to keep an eye on our younger son, James, as he might be worrying as he was working away from home. Although Nicholas appeared to be strong and was positive, I was aware that he too needed support. I held their hands while I silently prayed for them all. I then picked up a sheet of paper on which I had proclaimed in large letters "I LOVE YOU".

I had tried to bring our sons up to be independent so that they were at least capable of cooking and using a washing machine, but now I had to explain the essentials to Roger as he now had the unexpected problem of looking after himself quite apart from going to work, visiting me and answering the many messages left on our answer phone.

I attempted to make a list of people we

needed to let know about my condition, especially close family and friends. I was concerned about my work. I needed to let my headmistress know. I had been looking forward to teaching my new Form, especially as I had already taught the brothers and sisters of some of them, and I knew the children were expecting me to be there for them in September. Ironically, one of these children was the daughter of Tim Fooks, one of the GPs at my surgery, whom we knew also, together with his wife, Sarah, from church. I had known Peggy since she was a baby and had been looking forward to getting to know her better.

I felt so helpless having to leave so many tasks to Roger. I was optimistic that at least I would be able to help by writing several letters but how wrong I was. Whereas I used to enjoy letter-writing, to a certain extent, I was disappointed to find that I couldn't cope with it. I needed all my energy to communicate, through the written word, my thoughts and my basic needs to those around me.

5: MEDICAL SIDE OF ITU AND RESULTS

Immediately following the biopsy, I was completely dependent on the nurse allocated to me. That first one was very gentle. Nothing seemed to be too much trouble for her. One of her tasks was to wake me up at 2.15 a.m. to cough so that she could clear my tube. Unfortunately, I found it difficult to go back to sleep. The tracheostomy was causing me distress and we had to wait until 4.00 a.m. for the doctor to give permission for me to have morphine to ease my pain and enable me to sleep again. The disadvantage was that I became so drowsy I was forgetting to breathe some of the time, so it was a Catch 22 situation. I was beginning to understand that for every problem solved another invariably arose. On so many occasions a delicate balance has to be struck. Saying goodbye to the nurse at the end of the shift was like parting with an old and trusted friend. At every change-over a new relationship had to be developed. It was with relief that I came to realise that all the nurses in the unit had been highly trained and were extremely caring.

After visits by Mr. MacPherson, the physiotherapist and the anaesthetist, I was given an E.C.G. and, because St Richard's is a teaching hospital and my case was considered to be rare, close-up photographs were taken: two of my face and two inside my mouth. This gave me an insight into what it must have been like to be a freak at a fairground years ago. I had become an object of curiosity through no fault of my own. Understanding the reasons for this I duly obliged but the feeling was still there.

Rachel, the dietitian, came to see me and, after some discussion, she worked out exactly how many calories I should have according to my height, weight, level of activity and how much strength I would need. I told her that I wasn't too worried about my weight but that I was more interested in being fit which, on reflection, struck me as ironic and I couldn't help but be amused.

In the afternoon I was taken for a CT scan. The nurse put a dye into my bloodstream saying that it was to see if the blood flowed up my neck.

She warned me to expect to have diarrhoea afterwards. For the scan I had to lie on a flat surface which moved me back slowly into a tunnel.

"Since you cannot speak, lift your hand if you require the machine to stop for any reason, such as coughing or suctioning," the nurse explained. Congestion made lying on my back uncomfortable. I was finding it difficult to breathe as I was using a different tube and supply of oxygen. It would be a relief to go back to my original tube again.

On my return the nurse asked if I'd like to watch television. Countdown provided some mental stimulation followed by a programme about the Queen Mother to celebrate her ninety-ninth birthday. Through his Company our son, Nicholas, had been invited to her Birthday Lunch that day but ironically had had to decline as the Company had so much work that week. I was disappointed for him as it would have been an event to remember.

It was then that Mr. MacPherson arrived with the result of the biopsy. He'd heard that day, that the lump was a muco-epidermoid carcinoma which came from a saliva gland. It was therefore surprising that it was as far back as it was, just above the epiglottis. It would normally be slow growing, but it had not behaved according to type. As it had grown so rapidly during the previous week, Mr. MacPherson was wanting to get moving, as he put it, so that it didn't spread any further before treatment. It was very unusual.

6: FIRST TRIP TO GUILDFORD

When Roger arrived, I jotted down for him everything Mr. MacPherson had said. The scan on my neck had been clear, which was a good sign as this was the route that the cancer would be most likely to take. I still hoped that the lump wasn't going to spread into my larynx, or voice box. I thought I might eventually have a voice like the scientist, Stephen Hawking, and was concerned that it might frighten children.

Apparently, I'd been fitted with the best and most hygienic tracheostomy but there were others with a flap which allowed air to pass through the voice box to enable the patient to speak but Mr. MacPherson didn't want me to have one yet. He had decided to take me off the oxygen as it had a drying effect on my airway.

I had an appointment to see Dr. Stephen

Whitaker the following day. He had previously been a senior registrar at the Royal Marsden and was now Head of Oncology at the Royal Surrey County Hospital in Guildford. It was my understanding that I should go with the nurse, plus Roger, in an ambulance, if it weren't needed for an emergency. Mr. MacPherson told me that he would also be going. We were hoping that Dr. Whitaker would agree to some form of radio therapy treatment as it would give me a better quality of life than surgery alone.

That night was yet another with broken sleep. I slept from about 11.30 p.m. until 3 a.m., stayed awake until 6 a.m. then slept again until 7.40 a.m. when I was awoken by a crash in the ward. It felt strange in my mouth. It was hurting to swallow. Food seemed to be coming up from my stomach. I wondered if I should be sitting up more. The rate of food intake had been increased at 4 a.m. to fit in the required amount before the journey. I had been asked to buzz if I became bloated or felt sick.

Before I had even had a wash, Mr. MacPherson and Mr. Williams, another Maxillo Facial surgeon, arrived with a huge retinue mostly composed of students. I wrote a message saying, among other things, that I had lost the lid to my felt tip pen and was frightened the ink would dry up so that I would have no way of making people understand me. Possibly to explain the reason for my consternation and to my amazement, Mr. MacPherson told everyone that I was a very erudite patient. He certainly knew how to boost my morale. Understanding my predicament, both consultants agreed that I might eventually have a silver tracheostomy tube so that I could speak but I'd have to wait a while before having it fitted.

We were due to go to Guildford at 9 a.m. and at 8.55 a.m. the Head of ITU, Tony Conyers, came to see me. I was able to thank him for letting me stay there and for his kindness. I asked, using my writing pad, if the radiotherapy would 'cook' everything it was directed at or if it would be discriminatory. Unfortunately, the former was to be the case.

As we were rushed, I didn't have the planned painkiller before embarking on the journey. I had always imagined that ambulances were smooth and comfortable, but they are extremely bumpy and lurch tremendously with every bend in the road. Anyone who has travelled on a bus in the centre of Cairo, a city which Roger and I had recently visited, will be able to empathise. I now sat in a wheelchair, holding on for dear life, desperately longing for the journey to be over.

I felt very weak and thirsty. I had had Vaseline on my lips as they were so dry and now, in the ambulance, the nurse wet them for me. For some reason the ambulance driver went to the old St. Luke's Hospital before he realised that we were going to St. Luke's Cancer Centre at the Royal Surrey.

It was a relief to be out in the fresh air, albeit briefly, before going inside for our appointment. The nurse wheeled me into a small consulting room and waited outside the door. Roger and I were soon joined by Mr. MacPherson and Graham Smith, a registrar from St. Richard's. Mr. MacPherson introduced us to Dr. Whitaker who, similarly, was accompanied by a registrar. There were six of us and a wheelchair squeezed into a tiny room.

On meeting Dr. Whitaker, he asked about my immediate medical history. I was wishing I had had the painkiller as he did a nasendoscopy which I found uncomfortable. As soon as he saw my discomfort, Mr. MacPherson was quick to come to my aid. He was most compassionate. All the doctors present took it in turns to look into the nasendoscope. One of them explained to me that the lump in my throat was a funny shape. He told me that there were lots of bits like cells sticking up all over the place amidst a jelly-like mass.

Dr. Whitaker agreed that I should have a course of treatment. He explained what would happen and suggested that I come to Guildford as an in-patient, going home at weekends.

After Dr. Whitaker left, I wrote a note to Mr. MacPherson asking what I should do about my work. At that time, he envisaged I should possibly be returning to school after the autumn half term. I also told him about my niece's wedding, to be held on 14th August, as I was wondering whether I should have to miss it. I made it clear that I should like to go but that I was amazed at how weak I had been feeling on this particular day and recognised that it was of prime importance to get better.

Mr. MacPherson was instrumental in preparing me for the wedding. I was to have a PEG tube fitted for my feed to go directly into my stomach instead of via my nose and throat. While I was under a general anaesthetic for this, I should also have my tracheostomy changed to a different type so that I could speak more easily. I continued to write, asking if, when I had a silver tracheostomy, the metal might heat up during radiotherapy or whether it would be localised. I do not remember the answer, but I imagine we were moving one step at a time and that that would be dealt with when the time came. I continued to write, asking Mr. MacPherson if I would see him again once he'd handed me over to Dr. Whitaker, and he assured me that I would continue to be in his care regularly, for check-ups, for a long while.

After another tortuous ride in the ambulance, I felt weak and distressed by the time we arrived back in Chichester. I penned Sally, the nurse, a note saying that if she had been able to accompany me, she wouldn't have enjoyed the journey and the hospital had been hot and stuffy. It was much better here in ITU. I was relieved to be back in a comfortable bed. Mr. MacPherson had been keen to move me to a surgical ward as soon as possible. Knowing that a move was imminent, I wondered whether he would still come to see me wherever I happened to be.

My arm was now puffy. It had become very tender at Guildford, whilst I wasn't on the drip, and some blood had come into the tube. The nurse flushed it out. I felt hot. The trip to Guildford had exhausted me but had been productive. I was due to go there in about ten days for radiotherapy, but first I would have to make a couple of visits to have a mask fitted.

7: SEEING FAMILY

That night I was kept awake by one of the patients who was confused, a euphemism for shouting at everyone and telling them to go away. It was rather scary at first, but the nurses were very firm with him and eventually had to sedate him. Consequently, I was already awake when they moved me from ITU at 2.30 a.m. and took me to Wittering Ward. At 4.30 a.m. they checked my drip and at 6.30 a.m. my curtains were pulled back. It was a rude awakening as I had only just gone off to sleep.

The ward seemed extremely hot. I wondered if the food I had been having overnight might be making me feel extra warm. Saliva constantly built up in my mouth and I had to swallow it which I found most unpleasant. I had to force myself to do it. I wrote asking to have only a sheet over me so that I could be cooler. My lips were still dry, and I was thirsty.

The majority of patients in the ward appeared to be elderly. Listening to them speaking to one another reminded me of Alan Bennett's "Talking Heads". They innocently discussed the delights of being brought a cup of tea each morning, unaware of my frustration at being NIL BY MOUTH!

When I saw Nicky, my physio, I was still feeling exhausted from all the travelling the previous day and a sleepless night. As a result, I didn't seem to be managing to do all the recommended deep breaths even though I wanted to make good progress. I had been trying hard to keep cheerful, but this extreme tiredness made me tearful. Nicky was quick to reassure me that this was only to be expected in the circumstances. I needed to rest.

Not being able to speak to the others, I felt a bit isolated, but the nurses were kind, and I soon discovered the headphones for listening to the radio.

I wished I could have the opportunity to choose from the menu like everyone else. I missed the action of chewing and biting, quite apart from the taste and wonderful smell of food. It took me a long time to get used to not being able to eat meals.

I wished I could talk so that I could ring a few people. We were supposed to be having friends to stay for the coming weekend, but I was going to be in hospital. It was most frustrating.

The following morning, friends rang the hospital with their love and best wishes which lifted my spirits.

Cards came with every post and people sent me the most beautiful flowers of every colour and description. Initially I lost my sense of smell, but I could appreciate their appearance and the kindness of those who had sent them. I was soon to have visitors other than my immediate family which was a bonus. As well as coughing up blood and secretions I also needed to mop up the extra saliva so whenever anyone asked Roger what they could bring he always suggested tissues. I was using a box a day.

One of the highlights at this time was seeing my nephew, Philip, who had been teaching English in Japan and had returned home, briefly, for his sister's wedding. He had brought many interesting photographs to show me. I also enjoyed seeing Philip's sister, Helen, and her fiancé, Gary, catching some of their excitement as they discussed their plans. Together with my brother, Geoffrey, and his wife, Jennifer, we all prayed for one another.

Our younger son, James, had come home at

the weekend and brought his girlfriend, Verity, to see me. I told them what an excellent hospital St. Richard's was and brought them up to date with my news. We prayed together and James could no longer hide his emotions. It had been an enormous shock for my family, and I could not bear to see them suffering on my account. I tried to make them laugh, recalling the occasion when Beryl, a healthcare assistant, had put a blood pressure sleeve on me and it had blown up like a balloon, bursting off my arm with a flourish, causing us to go into hysterics. Her cheerfulness helped keep my spirits up many times. The emotions of sadness and elation frequently seemed to run side by side so that one's mood could change rapidly like quicksilver.

My family and I were trying to be positive and hoped that things would improve. I wrote to one of the nurses that I'd had a friend who had had cancer and that I remembered her saying,

"If fighting is the answer, then that's what I'm going to do."

She'd had such determination yet had succumbed. She had been a most caring person. Never having smoked, she had had lung cancer which must have been well developed. It had made me sceptical of the word fight. My friend, Liz, had had a strong faith. Shortly before she died, she said she felt God was holding her in the palm of his hand. Little did I know then that I, myself, would also experience such closeness during my own illness. I felt we didn't know what healing we were to have, whether spiritual or physical or both. I had always felt that when one prayed there would be a purpose behind whatever happened. I didn't know the answer and wondered if anyone did.

I had been lent a book by a friend, Annie, from our House Group. It was called "God's Plan for your Healing" by Colin Urquhart. I read it at every available opportunity and could hardly put it down. It was so relevant and gave me wonderful guidance on my spiritual journey.

8: SUDDEN CHANGE AND A STRUGGLE FOR BREATH!

When Mr. MacPherson asked me how I felt about my present condition I told him I just accepted it. I couldn't see the point in having any other response. He drew diagrams for me to explain about the new tracheostomy I was to have, which would allow air through my larynx to enable me to speak. The tumour's rapid growth during the previous week suggested that it could possibly be made up of two or even three different types, for example part of it might be a lymphoma which responds to chemotherapy. If this were the case it would mean having a mixture of treatments. They had to be sure.

On examining me early on Monday 9th August, Andrew Gilbert, the registrar, thought he heard a sound in my lower left lung. Although he said it was normal it gave me fresh determination to move around in order to clear it. During the morning I became frustrated that I had to sit still in the chair for so long because I was tied to the feeding machine. As soon as I was able, I walked along the corridor and out onto the balcony, a large, paved area with tubs of flowers. It was exhilarating to breathe in the cool, fresh air. I could even detect the smell of the sea.

Feeling brighter than I had for a long time, I returned to the ward.

At midday, I looked at my throat in the bathroom mirror but didn't like what I saw. I had noticed that my mouth and throat felt similar to the way they had when the tumour was growing rapidly. The Maxillo Facial Team was in Worthing that day so would be looking at my test results the following morning and deciding on the course of action.

By putting my finger over the hole in the tracheostomy tube, I had been able to speak thereby not having to rely on writing all the time. The doctors had been putting me under pressure to talk but I was always so pleased to have visitors that now I tended to be over enthusiastic and talked too much. Two or three days earlier one of the less experienced doctors had taken me off the humidifier, which conflicted with the advice I'd been given by the physiotherapists. I am sure he had meant well but it was probably too soon because my airway had become dry and now I was having difficulty breathing.

Sharon, an experienced physiotherapist, came to my aid. She was so gentle when she suctioned me that she managed to get up quite a bit of old blood. Her calm manner had caused me to relax. At some stage someone must have inadvertently scratched my trachea with the end of the tube because it frequently hurt, with the result that I had come to loathe the process intensely.

The sister in charge of the ward that night had helped nurse me in Intensive Care. She couldn't get the tube very far down because there seemed to be a blockage. The night was long and exhausting. I was struggling for air, which frightened me. I prayed to God to look after me and for the situation to be resolved.

At 8.30 a.m., to my relief, Mr. MacPherson arrived. I always tried to write notes for him in advance to save time and to make sure I didn't forget anything. He read my latest update and examined me. He looked concerned. As usual, he was thoughtful and decisive.

"We're not going to wait until tomorrow. We'll fit you into the list with another surgeon or doctor at 12.15 p.m. today, to have your tracheostomy tube changed."

During the morning, the large tube across my chest was making the most enormous rasping, groaning sounds. The nurses pulled the curtains around me for the doctors to examine me again and so that the nurses could suction me, thereby giving some measure of relief. I was thankful that soon I shouldn't have this painful struggle for breath.

I hoped my new trache' tube wouldn't be as dry and tickly as this one because I should have hated to have a coughing fit and ruin the wedding.

9: PEG AND ECLIPSE

On the Wednesday morning, 11th August, I received a visit from Mr. Bowyer, the surgeon who was going to perform the operation to insert my PEG tube. As Mr. Blake, his assistant, had done the previous day, Mr. Bowyer drew diagrams to show me exactly what to expect. He patiently answered my questions.

"Doctor Kendall, the anaesthetist, wants to try to put the tube down your throat first. Is that what you would like us to do?"

"Yes, please," I replied.

"We shall definitely try that first."

"The second option would be to go through the tummy button and another small hole. Whichever way we do it, it will remain in your stomach for between six weeks and twelve months and then you will have the tube changed."

"How would you do that?" I asked.

"We would cut the tube and it would disappear inside you. We would put a new one in and the old one would work its way through your intestines. I shall look forward to seeing you around eleven o'clock."

"DURING THE ECLIPSE!" I was aghast.

"It will only take ten minutes," he retorted.

"Will I be awake again by then?"

His reply came quickly,

"I'll do the operation after the Eclipse so that we can both see it."

"Thank you."

My disappointment had turned to elation when Mr. Bowyer had told me that my operation would be put back so that no-one would miss the Eclipse. It was to be the first Solar Eclipse seen from this country since 1927 – a rare occurrence! Feeling thrilled and carrying my special glasses, bought for the occasion, I was ready for my usual walk on the balcony but, just as I was turning the door handle to go outside, I was arrested by the voice of a nurse behind me,

"STOP!" she ordered, "You are not allowed outside. Only hospital staff are allowed out on the balcony." I could hardly believe it. I had been actively encouraged to go out there until this moment and it was almost always deserted, yet when I wanted to be out there most of all I wasn't allowed to. I felt bitterly disappointed.

I had been looking forward to experiencing the eeriness of it: the darkening of the sky, the chill and the lack of birdsong. I couldn't even get low enough to see the Eclipse through the window. I had to content myself with watching it, second-hand, on television.

Patrick Moore, the astronomer, was also somewhat disappointed, as it was cloudy from his particular spot in Cornwall. We later heard that the view of it had been perfect from the part of Cornwall where we had booked our holiday especially for this event, but it was not to be.

At the appointed time, I'd had a wash and was wearing a clean hospital gown. The porter arrived to wheel me to the Operating Theatre. As we approached it, the now familiar figure of Mr. Bowyer stepped forward to greet me.

"Well, what did you think of the Eclipse?" he enquired innocently.

"I wasn't allowed out on the balcony to see it," I wrote. His reaction was one of amazement,

"Why ever not?"

"The nurse who stopped me said it was a 'management decision'," I explained.

Sure enough, Mr. Bowyer was as surprised as I had been. The surgeons I have met are more understanding than whoever is responsible for the petty rules and regulations. I had an ally but it was too late. I had missed a once in a lifetime experience. I was glad that Mr. Bowyer, himself, had been able to witness the event and was thankful that his thoughtfulness had, at least, enabled me to see it live on television.

The operation to fit the PEG tube took from about 11:45am until 12:10pm. I opened my eyes in Recovery at ten minutes to one. Dr. Kendall, the anaesthetist, came and spoke to me,

"Everything has gone well so far. We were able to put the tube down your throat as we'd hoped. Mr. Bowyer was very pleased."

10: VISIT TO THE MOULD ROOM AT GUILDFORD

My memories of being fitted for a mask are mostly pleasant. The only disadvantage, as far as I was concerned, was that it involved quite lengthy periods lying on a couch flat on my back, so it was reassuring that I had a nurse assigned to my welfare who would come to my aid if I needed any help with the tracheostomy tube and could help me should I have breathing problems. A chair was provided for her so that she could observe my progress.

The people at the Mould Room were most considerate towards me, when they saw the problem, and were quick to alleviate the situation. They supported my back and provided a curved block to hold my head and neck at a comfortable angle. Once I was in position on the couch, they deftly set to work. They covered my face and neck with something like Vaseline, to protect my skin. After this they swathed the prepared area with lovely, warm bandages, soaked in either latex or plaster of Paris; I cannot remember which, yet I do recall the luxurious feeling of being warm and cared for. The mask was to cover my nose, but an airway had been left so that air could enter the tracheostomy tube.

We had to wait for the bandages to dry as they were to form the prototype for the plastic mask itself. Everything had to be very precise, so I had been asked to look at a certain mark on the ceiling and hold my head perfectly still while they took the necessary measurements. They were skilful and soon they were removing the newly formed prototype, bearing my likeness, before cleansing my skin, which felt most therapeutic. The nurse was a lovely person called Jill, who said she would look out for me when I came for treatment. I thanked the two members of staff, who had both been so gentle with me, and it was arranged for me to return for the fitting and to make any adjustments.

I was really looking forward to seeing them again.

11: HELEN'S WEDDING DAY!

My two clocks had fallen on the floor during the night, so I was unaware of the time. I pressed the button for the nurse. It was Saturday 14th August, the day of my niece's Wedding. Adding to my list, the nurse brought me the rest of the items I would require: more tissues, nursing towels, cardboard dish, bottles of food, spare tube for the tracheostomy, instructions for the drip, instructions for the tracheostomy care, suctioning equipment and instructions and gauze for cleaning the PEG opening (stoma site).

Roger, James and Verity arrived as Verity, who was a recently qualified physiotherapist, was going to be responsible for me during the wedding that day and had agreed to meet Nicky, my physio, to go through procedures together and ask any questions before we left the hospital.

We were waiting for Pharmacy to send up their package before we were free to leave.

The journey passed quickly. Once we were at home, I tried on the outfit I'd worn to Nicholas and Penny's wedding. To my astonishment, it fitted without any discomfort around the waist. Although my stomach seemed to stick out, I had generally lost weight, so I was able to wear normal clothes after all. What a blessing! I could even wear a hat.

The next thing I recall is going into the church on Roger's arm, with James and Verity walking behind. It had not been definite whether I would make it or not so to see the expressions of sheer delight on the faces of my dear brother and sister-in-law, Geoffrey and Jennifer, and also the rest of our family was amazing. We were made to feel so welcome that it was a moment I shall always treasure. We had been told only a matter of days before that I had cancer, so it was still a shock to everyone. There was so much love there that day. We were all on an emotional high.

My niece, Helen, looked amazing. I don't think she stopped smiling all day. Her new husband, Gary, was on fine form, too. Gary was a worship leader and some of his friends were playing at the Wedding. The music was lovely. The atmosphere was wonderful. The singing was beautiful and sincere. Young friends stood around the couple and prayed for them and both their pastors made the Wedding very special.

After the Service, during the photo shoot, we had the opportunity to mingle, catching up with people we knew and being introduced to those we hadn't met before. Eventually, it was time to go to the reception.

Having been in hospital for several days, it was wonderful to be in the outside world again. Verity accompanied me to a room which had been laid aside for my use. The family helped transport my equipment from the car and we quickly sorted out my nebuliser and made sure everything was at hand. We joined the others for the Wedding Breakfast, sitting in the middle near the front, fairly close to the top table. I took advantage of being able to speak through my latest tracheostomy tube. It made a welcome change to be able to have normal conversations with a variety of people, without the common denominator of illness.

It was in a break during the meal, that I received a gentle tap on the shoulder, and I turned round to find Alan, Helen's pastor, bending towards me. He suggested that he and the other pastor and I find a quiet corner and asked if I would like them to pray for me. I was thrilled. I said yes immediately. I had been hoping they might do that.

I had been trying to speak as much as possible but now I had to stop. The speaking tube was slightly longer than the other thus irritating my trachea and I had been coughing blood. My throat was itching a lot, so I changed the tracheostomy tube to the non-speaking one.

My brother, Geoffrey, made a deeply moving speech and Gary's was amusing, followed by the hilarious speeches of his two Best Men! It was a terrific double act; they even used a projector and screen. I had to cling on to my tummy throughout the time they were speaking. Everyone was laughing almost non-stop.

After the speeches, Geoffrey announced that, while the dance band was being set up, a group of us would be going into a side room where the two pastors were going to lead prayers for me. All the close family, including Helen and Gary, and several others joined us. From the outset, one of the pastors asked anyone who did not believe to leave the room. Their prayers were powerful. I remember sitting on a chair in the middle of the room with tears streaming down my face as I was confessing my sins. I had to do it silently as I was unable to speak with this particular tube. Jennifer was in front of me, praying and reassuring me. I remember her gently wiping away my tears. Most people prayed and after a while, they left to join the dancing.

Jennifer and possibly others, whom I couldn't see, remained in that room for quite a long time. It had been such a privilege that they had been willing to do this. It meant everything to me because I knew they had genuine faith.

Verity had looked after me well, but we wanted her to be able to enjoy herself with James and the other young guests. We wandered onto the dance floor to see everyone having fun before saying our goodbyes and expressing our thanks.

The next thing I knew, Roger and I were strolling along the corridor to Wittering Ward. We were both feeling on cloud nine. It had been an amazing day, far exceeding our expectations. As we approached the staff desk, the nurses on duty got up and came towards us. It was quite late in the evening, so the ward was quiet. They were not only very complimentary about my outfit, but they couldn't get over how well I looked. Roger was thrilled to tell them all about it. It had been the best medicine possible.

12: TRANSITION TIME!

On Monday 16th August, I had my next appointment at Guildford at 2.45pm to have the mask fitted. Geoffrey and Jennifer visited me and prayed that I wouldn't have a bad journey to Guildford but that it would be comfortable. As the time passed I was becoming increasingly concerned about getting to my appointment. No-one else seemed at all worried, which I thought was strange. This was one occasion when I found my inability to speak particularly frustrating. At 2.20pm. I was still waiting. I wrote a message for the nurse in charge, asking if someone could alert the people in the Mould Room at Guildford to the situation. I was assured that this would be done but I later learned that the message hadn't got through and they had been expecting to see me.

Roger arrived on the Tuesday morning, as planned, to take me home. It was reassuring to have him at my side instead of having to relay everything backwards and forwards second or third hand. I wrote a few notes for him to read, finally informing him that,

'The ambulance didn't turn up yesterday, so I missed my appointment. There is another fixed for Friday. The beginning of the treatment has been postponed from 25th to 31st August.'

Roger could scarcely believe this.

"I could have driven you there myself if I'd known," he sputtered. I could sense his frustration at these hindrances. To avoid any further delays it was agreed that Roger should take me to my next appointment in the car, which would indeed be more comfortable.

13: BEING MEASURED FOR RADIOTHERAPY

Bang! Bang! Bang! Bang! The shots rang through my ears so loudly I thought my head would explode. A man moved around me deftly as he fired bolts through the plastic shell covering my lower face and neck so that I was fastened to the block on which I lay. I was lying in the centre of an enormous darkened room. Suddenly, I was alone.

"Keep as still as you can and try hard not to swallow. If you need to be suctioned, lift your hand and we'll come."

The harder I tried not to swallow the more I wanted to. I was willing the tickle in my throat not to become unbearable. All the secretions from my nose were collecting in my throat by force of gravity. "O Lord, please help me to bear this."

X-rays were taken to ascertain the exact size and location of my tumour. Having worked this out, the radiologists came and made various marks on my mask indicating the exact area that they wanted to treat.

Initially, it was thought that I should have treatments every day until I'd had twenty in total. The Bank Holiday would be missed but added on to the end and, similarly, if the machines needed servicing. I would be in the room for 10 minutes at a time and would have it coming from three different directions.

As I lay prostrate during this procedure, thoughts ran through my head: 'If the tumour changes in size will they continue to target the same area? Will they take further x-rays to check the size of the tumour as we go along? If they don't take further x-rays how will they know how quickly the tumour is shrinking?'

Once it was completed, I was released. I could sit up, cough and, best of all, be FREE.

14: HELPFUL ADVICE FROM THE ONCOLOGY REGISTRAR

It was later, while Roger and I were at The Royal Surrey Hospital, waiting outside the radiography unit for the final preparations for the radiotherapy, that we were joined by Dr. Alison Falconer, who was delightful. She was one of Dr. Whitaker's registrars and proceeded to explain, not only what was about to take place, but went on to discuss with us many things we hadn't even considered. She made it clear that she thought that as I would be resident at the hospital during the week for most probably six and a half weeks, I should be given a room of my own and wear my own clothes during the day. I should think of it as a hostel rather than a hospital. I would be able to go down to the Radiography Unit for my treatment each day and she suggested that I might like to go to the Fountain Centre, a Day Unit which was run by volunteers and was a place where I would be able to relax and receive complimentary therapies. This sounded promising.

The doctors were afraid that I might become institutionalised, which can be a danger when one has a long course of treatment.

Among the things Dr. Falconer urged us to consider was the possibility of giving up my job. We both looked at her aghast. That had never occurred to us. She was serious,

"You are about to have the longest course of treatment possible for your condition. It is like a microwave; the cooking time is twice as long because it carries on after treatment has finished. Radiotherapy makes you feel very tired which can continue for quite a long time afterwards. I think you should consider this carefully. It's surprising how many people do have to go down to one salary. I'm sure you would manage."

It's amazing how quickly one's life can change. One moment I had a few symptoms, the next we were talking about my giving up work – such a huge part of my life!

It was particularly interesting that Dr. Falconer thought that the tumour would have been growing for about eighteen months, which happened to tie in exactly with my exposure to a strong-smelling carpet glue, which had left a foul taste on the back of my tongue, lasting for hours a day for several days. It had been so ghastly that I had said, at the time,

"If I have cancer one day, I shall know the reason why."

Little did I know that this is exactly what was to happen. We should not speak these things over ourselves.

15: TIME AT HOME BEFORE RADIOTHERAPY

After the biopsy at St. Richard's, I had been sent home for a fortnight to build up my strength before embarking on the full course of radiotherapy at The Royal Surrey at Guildford. The days were warm and sunny, so we rested together out in the garden. Roger had put out the soft garden chairs and moved the small wrought iron table across to me so that I could still admire the beautiful flowers, placed on it, which people had so kindly sent. The abelia bush nearby was in bloom and the greengages were ripening each day; Roger picked me a few to taste. Friends popped round to see us, all of which helped make it a special time.

I could understand his reasons in many ways, but I was still amazed that Roger was prepared to sleep in the same room as me, let alone share the same bed. I was having to nebulise, cough up secretions and put the light on at intervals during the night apart from which, the tumour exuded an unpleasant odour, which I, myself, was unable to detect. Formerly, I had had an extremely strong sense of smell, but I seemed to have lost it. Perhaps this was beneficial. On reflection, it must have been associated with having a tracheostomy; after all, the air was rarely passing through my nostrils.

We had the pleasure of being visited by my district nurse, who turned out to be an old friend, Bridget Vickerstaff. Bridget was most professional and was a great comfort to me. She was strict about hygiene and changed my dressings expertly. I felt exceptionally well cared for.

During this time at home, we tried to contact old friends who would have no other way of knowing what had happened. I managed to write a few letters while Roger continued to cope with the many telephone messages. At least the pressure of so much travelling each day was off for a while and we could enjoy relaxing in our garden together.

It was at this time that my brother and sister-in law's church asked if I should like a group of them to come and pray for me at home. Roger and I were absolutely delighted that they had asked and welcomed them with hugs of gratitude.

We took them into the sitting room where we offered tea and biscuits. Soon everyone was settled. They were very friendly and there was a good atmosphere. The prayer time began. Verses from Scripture were read out and people spoke in turn as they were led by the Holy Spirit. At one point, I was asked to kneel down in the middle and all the women were asked to lay hands on me, although everyone could still pray.

It was while we were doing this that I remember being acutely aware of the presence of Jesus in front of me. I had my eyes closed yet I could see His robe and his feet; I couldn't see His face, yet I knew that it was Him; then I saw Him gently put his hands against my throat, slightly to the left. I could feel tremendous warmth emanating from His hands. I didn't want to move in case He left. It was the most wonderful, peaceful experience. I was unaware of the passage of time, but it must have been getting late because some people had to go. One of the elders drew me up on to the sofa. I told him, "Jesus is here. I'm frightened to move in case He goes away." I wanted to stay where I was all night, even forever; there was such an amazing sense of peace and well-being. I had never experienced anything like this before and I didn't want it to end.

My sister-in-law, Jennifer, told me later, that on their way home, the elder who had drawn me up on to the sofa said he had thought, at first, that I would have a miracle but during the evening, God had told him that I would be healed but it would be a fairly long, gentle process. Earlier in the evening, I had been trying to conquer any doubts, but now I knew with certainty that my healing had begun.

16: TREATMENT BEGINS

My first radiotherapy session had been booked for 31st August at 1.40 pm so, having been advised to arrive there twenty minutes early, Roger and I checked to make sure we hadn't forgotten anything and set off in the car to Guildford in good time.

On arrival at the Chilworth Ward, at the Royal Surrey Hospital, I was taken to the second bed on the left, the same as at St. Richard's! Roger and I went down to L1 at St. Luke's Cancer Centre for my radiotherapy session at 1.20pm for 1.40pm only to be told that the machine was broken but that this was most unusual. There were two different types of machine and two of each of these, so only one other machine was right for me and that was fully booked!

The head radiographer, Helen Chessman, warned us that the treatment would cause it to become very sore and dry both inside and outside my mouth and that I would become very tired as time went on. After our chat, Helen kindly arranged for my radiotherapy treatment to be fitted in at 4.50pm. which she would do herself with her assistant.

That night, on the ward, there was a lot of coughing, moaning, visiting the bathroom and other disturbances. I had to clean my tube. We were all apologizing for waking one another up and for the general restlessness.

At 7am I got up and nebulised. I had washed but was still dressing when I was called for radiotherapy. I walked down with Helen whom I'd met the previous day, but ……Aargh! We were talking when, all of a sudden, I felt the tumour against the back of my throat and I couldn't stop the gagging reaction. Helen let me rest a little while before asking,

"Do you want to go ahead now or wait until later in the day?"

"I'll carry on because it could easily happen again," I replied.

I thought it would be better lying on my back but the mask fitted so tightly, pressing on my throat and chest, that I felt as though I couldn't even swallow. They were very understanding and were doing it as efficiently as they could. Helen told me,

"You are probably sensitive and are having a reaction by swelling after the first day's treatment. I'll ring the doctor and ask him to give you anti-inflammatories to reduce the swelling."

Greg Hart, the lovely doctor who had examined me on arrival on the ward, spoke to Dr. Whitaker who prescribed steroids. Greg had been on duty all day and was also on duty all night, when he had three emergencies to deal with; then he had to work half a day the following day, which meant he was working until 5pm! I felt it shouldn't be allowed.

The next morning, my radiotherapy went much better than the previous day. At Greg's suggestion, I jotted down a list of questions to ask Dr. Whitaker, who was due to come round between 1 and 2 o'clock. After the consultation, I wanted to go outside but Greg told me I was anaemic so I would have to have a blood transfusion that afternoon, so I waited around. After a while, they said I'd have it for ten hours overnight!

At 6.30pm the blood was ready. I had a 70% haemoglobin count and they liked it to be no less than 100%. I was to have three units, which would take four hours each. June, a fellow patient, said that if the blood were to flow too quickly, you could have a heart attack! I hardly slept and if I did drop off, I seemed to be woken up to have my blood pressure checked every hour!

Dr. Whitaker was concerned that my stomach had been bleeding more than was evident, maybe from the operation or from the Voltarol so he changed that to paracetamol, which would go straight into my stomach via the PEG and gave me Zoton to neutralize the acid.

17: FINDING INSPIRATION

Whenever I could, I took my book, Colin Urquhart's 'God's Plan for your Healing', and walked outside to sit on the grass. The sun was still quite strong so I put a handkerchief over the sensitive area of skin. I didn't realise, at first, that I had to protect even the back of my neck. It was a time to think and to enjoy the beautiful, warm sunshine. It was a time of relaxation and blessing. Between 1 and 2pm. it was Quiet Time on the ward. Everyone had had their lunch and visitors didn't arrive until 2 o' clock so it was an opportunity for patients to lie down and rest, even to sleep but it was understood that no one talked unless it was absolutely necessary. It was a special part of the day for both patients and staff.

I was disappointed to learn that Dr. Whitaker came round on a Thursday and that I had missed him because I had been having my radiotherapy. Perhaps I would have to ask the radiographers to fit me in earlier on a Thursday so that I could be there when he came next time. I had seen his rear view along the corridor as I was being wheeled back from my treatment. Greg together with Julia, who had come from the Royal Marsden, saw to me instead.

On Friday 10th September, I was given two doses of senna, a laxative, which caused me to have such terrible pain that I hardly knew how to bear it. My son James arrived, at this point, to take me home and was shocked to find me like this. He held my hand and sat with me while we waited for the doctor. The pain was coming in waves. James's presence was a great comfort to me. When Greg came, he immediately gave me an injection to counteract the effect of the senna. My body was having to get used to the liquid feed.

Time at home was precious; the weekend passed all too quickly.

Back on the ward, a wonderful nun called Marianne came to see me.

"I see you are reading a book by Colin Urquhart," Marianne commented. I was unable to speak because of the swelling in my throat but, writing in my pad, I told her more.

Art Therapy at the St. Luke's Cancer Centre

went well. I felt very relaxed and met several people. We shared experiences. My partner in the Art Class was a teacher of young ones but had given up work. She had three children aged sixteen, twelve and nine. She'd had Melanoma for three years. Now, it had flared up in her abdomen again.

We painted pictures inspired by listening to readings or music, such as Vaughan-Williams' "The Lark Ascending" played on the violin by David Oistrakh, and a conversation in paint without using words. We all wanted to do it again.

It was whilst attending Art Therapy, that we were given a copy of part of President Nelson Mandela's Inaugural Speech which I found most inspiring. On his death, both the TV and Radio broadcast the voices of many all over the world, whether world leaders or ordinary people, who were affected by his humility, compassion and work for justice. One person commented on his warmth and sense of confidence, expecting that when he walked into a room people would like him. Immediately, I remembered the words from his speech: "We do not have the right not to shine."

18: TREATMENT CONTINUES

The following Monday, 20th September, Roger brought me in for midday to find that I had been given a room of my own.

That evening I watched a remarkably interesting programme on TV on Private Health Care versus the NHS. Dame Emma Nicholson's husband had been in a private hospital in London, and it had been an absolute disaster. His tracheostomy tube had become blocked, and he had been starved of oxygen for fifteen minutes; he had had a heart attack and died. She was saying that if he had been in a National Health Hospital, he would have had a better chance because there are more doctors on duty during the night and that in an emergency, the private hospitals have to rely on NHS Intensive Care.

I made a timetable in my notepad, so that I

could arrange my visits to the Fountain Centre around the radiotherapy treatments, doctors' rounds and my visitors. The family usually came two or three evenings between them and several of my colleagues from school came along after work. I was thrilled to see them and to hear all their news. Once term began, it felt very strange not to be a part of it but everyone there was wonderful. Our school had always had a family feel to it and I had worked closely with my colleagues for several years. They were good friends and couldn't have been more supportive. The parents, too, were tremendously kind and thoughtful. I thought of the children constantly, wondering what they were doing. I really missed them.

One day, I was surprised to have a visit from the Chairman of the Governors. I had also taught her children so I knew her quite well, but I was very touched that she should be making this effort to come and see me. She suggested that I might like to take the year off so that I would be able to recuperate properly and even offered my husband and me the chance to stay in their holiday home on an island near Vancouver Island. This was very exciting and gave me something to look forward to. Mary's idea was that I would then come back to school refreshed and well. She showed me photographs to whet my appetite. I couldn't get over her generosity.

Having a television in my room, I watched all the cookery programmes I could, copying down the recipes with every intention of preparing these dishes once I had returned home. My fascination with food seems to have been a psychological way of dealing with my 'real food' deprivation. The more I could see and smell it, the better.

When Roger and Nicholas came that evening, I accompanied them to the restaurant, where we could sit together and I could have a few sips of soup. I liked it but I couldn't manage to drink it very well.

That night I couldn't sleep because my tongue was very sore. I took painkillers at 5.30am as I couldn't last any longer, but I had to wait another twelve hours for the Zoton (stomach liner) as it had to be sent up from Pharmacy. Everything was so SLOW.

Having not seen him on the previous two Thursdays, I was pleased that Dr. Whitaker did come on 23rd. He arranged for me to have stronger painkillers. He also changed the laxative and reduced the number of steroids as he considered they were no longer needed so much.

I had been trained to be as independent as possible, but the disadvantage was that the staff thought I could do everything and so forgot to change my PEG dressing. It usually became infected while I was here so the district nurse, at home, had sent me back with a couple of suitable dressings as the hospital seemed to be short of everything. After taking a swab of the PEG site for Dr. Whitaker, a nurse called Doreen always made a point of changing my dressings whenever she was on duty, for which I was most grateful.

During my weekend at home, on Sunday, 26th September, Roger and I went, together with James and Verity, to lunch with our friends Louise and James Mursell and their family. I had to decline the first course but, for dessert, Louise gave me a bowl of the most gorgeous red jelly and vanilla ice cream. It slipped down so well that I even had a second helping. It was particularly memorable because after that, I was unable to swallow any more solid food; there wasn't enough room in my throat. Louise's mother, Stella, had been the first to be aware, originally, that something might be seriously wrong. It was so good to see them again.

When I next saw Dr. Whitaker, he explained that I would have the tumour looked at and examined. It would probably be removed about four weeks after the end of the radiotherapy treatment. Rather than shrink, the majority of cells would die. I would need to have it all removed. I should still be able to swallow afterwards. My tracheostomy could just be taken out and a sticky dressing put over it and it would heal itself. The hospital would tell the district nurses all that had happened, and they would decide when to change any medication.

Dr. Whitaker wanted me to have all thirty-three treatments. He thought there was bound to be a lump still there as it was such a 'slow-growing' tumour so he thought an operation was highly likely. It would possibly take place in mid-November, probably at St. Richard's on Mr. MacPherson's own ward. Mr. MacPherson needed to see me to book the operation so 14th October would be a good time to see them both.

19: TOWARDS THE END OF THE TREATMENT

My birthday fell near the beginning of October. On the previous day, my colleagues at school had brought me folders full of cards made by the children and arrangements of flowers, including some from parents. Without their thoughtfulness there wouldn't have been the same joy that day because everything that came in the post took four days to reach me. The hospital delivery service evidently wasn't a priority.

I woke up at 6am. on the day, in eager anticipation. I read each card carefully, remembering every person in turn. Doing this absolutely made my day. It was a really special birthday. My friend, Pam, who taught Art, had made silk cushions with the children. My old form had designed one based on the weather as they had particularly enjoyed learning about that with me, so Pam told me later. They had painted a yellow, smiling sun, a puffy white cloud in a blue sky with a beautiful rainbow below. It is something I shall always treasure. The significance of the rainbow was not lost on me. It means that God keeps His promises, which meant everything to me and still does.

After opening the cards, I turned my attention to the gorgeous bouquets of flowers. I was quite overwhelmed. Some children and a friend had given me soft toys, one being a rabbit and the other a striped cat, which were fun. It gave me great pleasure to arrange everything around the room and to think of all those dear people who had sent such kindness to me at a time when I needed it most.

Roger came that evening with Geoffrey and Jennifer. Jennifer took photographs, which showed us beaming for the camera. In fact, I was glowing; it was such a day of love.

After the euphoria of my birthday celebrations, I found the fifth week to be the worst psychologically. I had been keeping cheerful until then but suddenly I found it really hard. I think this is probably because my throat had become extremely sore and I was fairly isolated, being in a room on my own. A lot of my friends had already gone home, so it could be lonely, and it was difficult to deal with the pain during the small hours, waiting for the medication to arrive.

By contrast, the sixth week was one of the best because, as well as knowing that the Treatment was almost over, I was on a ward again with other women who were such a laugh it took my mind off the pain. They say that laughter is the best medicine and it certainly helped us. The one who made us laugh most was Jean, a lady who was very ill. After she had gone home there were a lot of tears because she had made everyone feel special.

All the others in this ward, including Jean, were having chemotherapy. They came into hospital for two to three days every three weeks, so there had grown quite a bond between them. I felt I was missing out in a way, yet I felt sorry for them because I knew that I was going to get well whereas their futures weren't all as optimistic. The lady in the bed opposite mine always had perfect make-up and looked glamorous but informed me that she had been told she wouldn't recover. I was shocked; she looked so well. The lady at the end to my right was interested to see that I was reading a book by Colin Urquhart because she, too, was reading one of his books called 'My Dear Child'. She said it touched her so much that it made her cry. She recommended it to me.

Yet again, while I was on a ward, I found it a good opportunity to pray for the other patients, particularly if I lay awake at night. Several patients had secondaries, which was very sad. Some people had tumours cropping up all over the place. There seemed to be a lot with breast cancer. The treatment seemed to depend on the type of tumour and its position.

I was now writing to everyone as my main form of communication. On Monday, 11th October I could no longer speak. I had started to lose my voice two to three weeks previously and I was about to embark on the final three treatments. Dr. Whitaker said that any more would cause damage, which we wouldn't want.

On the morning of 14th October, I had woken at 6:30. I needed to take my Oramorph but had no water, so the nurse took the jugs to get some. At 7:45am the drugs trolley still hadn't arrived. My face and head were burning hot. It felt so good when I put very cold hands on my skin and eyelids. My throat was still painful every time I swallowed my saliva. The drugs trolley, which normally came at 6:30 didn't arrive until 9am. When I went for my treatment at 8:20 am, I had needed the steroid because when they put the mask on, it made me gag all the time and I was coughing up blood and mucus. I wasn't fit enough for my treatment until much later.

Roger arrived that morning for the expected meeting with Dr. Whitaker and Mr. MacPherson, so I explained to him that we had been held up. We went along to the waiting area where, eventually, we found out that, although the nurse had put my name on the list, my name wasn't on the computer so Mr. MacPherson didn't know and was on his way back to St. Richard's. Dr. Whitaker was extremely busy so we knew we had to be back on the ward to see him at 2pm. Roger was upset that we wouldn't be seeing Mr. MacPherson that day.

The radiotherapy treatment was now completed. I had had six and a half weeks of thirty-three sessions. On his ward round, Dr. Whitaker told us that we were to have a joint meeting with Mr. MacPherson in four weeks to give the tumour a little more 'cooking' time and that I would be having a Magnetic Imaging Scan at The King Edward VII Hospital at Midhurst. He went on to say, "The radiotherapy may kill 90% of the tumour but it might not necessarily go away. It was already big at the back of the tongue and it may not shrink at all because it was so slow growing. Its roots go deep into the base of the tongue. We still have to see what happens in the six weeks after treatment."

20: RETURNING HOME AFTER RADIOTHERAPY TREATMENT

I returned home on Friday 15th October. Doctor Nichols, from the St. Barnabas' Hospice in Worthing, came to assess me. Apparently, the next two weeks were going to be the worst, so he advised me to gradually increase the painkiller each time and that, once things started to improve, I would be able to reduce the dosage thereby also eliminating certain side effects.

He told us about St. Barnabas' Hospice, explaining that hospice care and palliative medicine had come on in leaps and bounds. They now looked at the whole picture: emotional and family. After informing us about the hospice, itself, he gave us information of immediate relevance,

"There's a team of nurses who visit people

regularly to discuss change, any issues and to be kept up to date. They are all very senior nurses with training and counselling skills and have knowledge of different treatments and drugs. They are a good source of support and information, working alongside the district nurses."

Soon after this, I had a visit from Rosie Wookie, one of the nursing team mentioned by Dr. Nichols. She was a very caring person and it was her priority to help me with pain control and to ask questions about Roger, Nicholas and James to make sure their needs were being met. I was pleased she was including them in her area of concern. Rosie continued to ask about them on subsequent visits. She was most professional yet immediately felt like a good friend.

She went through every item of medication, asking detailed questions about the effects of each one, studying the various doses and looking at everything from many angles. Rosie's advice was always wise and her visits were most welcome.

I had told Rosie that it had been most reassuring for me to have the district nurse regularly, which gave continuity. It was having someone, apart from the surgeon, of course, who had known what was going on all the way through, which helped enormously. I had also told Rosie that my faith was invaluable, and that I had learned a lot through meeting the many cancer patients at Guildford and communicating with them. This whole experience had been like living in another world – all a bit unreal.

21: MRI SCAN AND MEETING

Roger took me for an MRI Scan at the King Edward VII Hospital in Midhurst, West Sussex, which was a grand old Hospital set in beautiful grounds not far from where we live. Magnetic Imaging was considered to be a safer method of seeing what was going on inside than having an X-ray. It seemed less stressful than the CAT scan I'd had originally but that could be because I was more used to these things by that time. Whereas my memory of the CAT scan was of a bright, well-lit room, the King Edward VII seemed darker and quieter. I seem to remember a notice warning me not to ask the operator questions.

I remember lying on my back but my memory of the actual process is now vague. I think the machine moved along taking images of the area so that the size of the tumour could be assessed.

I saw these images coming up on the screen or wall ahead of me but they did not mean anything to me.

Beforehand, Roger had been given a piece of paper saying, 'Please do not ask the radiologist the results. These have to be interpreted by the consultant.' Roger thought, 'That's a pity,' and waited while they did the scan. Afterwards the operator said,

"That's good." By this remark, Roger thought it meant that I was OK but I thought it meant that the images were clear.

Soon after this we were at the Royal Surrey again, sitting in front of Dr. Whitaker and Mr. MacPherson, whose seriousness was matched by the grave expressions on their faces. This was in complete contrast to my optimism. The radiotherapy hadn't worked; I was in the 1% whose tumour didn't respond to the treatment. They told me that the tumour hadn't shrunk but had stayed the same. They seemed to be so troubled by the outcome of the radiotherapy that it came as a shock to me that they were so worried. I understood what they were telling me but I knew that I was going to be well.

I had been prayed for and Brian from Cowfold Church had been given a prophetic word that I would receive my healing, so all along I was confident that I was going to recover. The doctor and the surgeon did not know the reason for my optimism and seemed to think that what they were saying hadn't sunk in as I still remained calm.

I remember particularly Dr. Whitaker being surprised that I had no voice and asking me, "Why can't you speak?"

I thought, 'It's the radiotherapy which caused my voice to go hoarser and hoarser until it disappeared. The radiologists had told me. Why didn't he know this?'

Roger helped explain what had happened.

When Dr. Whitaker had been doing the rounds a few days earlier, I had written a note for him telling him that I had lost my voice. Having read it he had told me it would return in three to four weeks so he must have forgotten this or thought it should have come back already.

I had had the maximum amount of radiotherapy. They told us that major surgery was now the only option.

22: ANOTHER BIOPSY AND MAJOR SURGERY

Thus, I received a letter informing me that I was to have another surgeon, Mr. Williams, who was to carry out the main operation and, prior to that, a biopsy at Worthing Hospital, on 6th December 1999. We didn't realise who he was and rang the hospital, in indignation, to ask why I wouldn't be having Mr. MacPherson. We neither knew, at that point, that the surgeons worked as a team, nor did we realise that I was being passed onto him because Mr. John Williams was the most experienced surgeon.

As things were, it was thought that I would have to have my voice box removed as well as a large area of my tongue, but Mr. Williams had had previous experience of operating on a tumour like mine, which hadn't responded to radiotherapy. After removing the tumour, he had frozen the residual area with liquid nitrogen, a process called cryotherapy, and believed he could save my voice box by freezing my tongue in the same way.

Surprisingly, the ward at Worthing Hospital to which I was admitted was almost empty, so I had a choice of beds. I chose to be in a room of my own so that I could administer my medicines more easily and enjoy a degree of privacy. I was taking twelve different types of drug at that time so I had drawn up a chart with dates, times and boxes so that I could tick them off as I took them. It was no use relying on my memory, especially when some of them had to be taken on alternate days or some had to be taken four times a day and others twice. I had bought a large plastic box, with a lid, especially for them as I had different size syringes to look after as well. It meant I could transport them easily between home and hospital as well as keeping them dust free. The nurses seemed amazed at my charts, but I don't think I could have coped as well otherwise.

The building was new and, because there was a lull, the nurses had time to come and talk to me.

I remember Mr. Williams coming to introduce himself before the biopsy when he explained what would happen. I don't remember much else until afterwards when I had been moved to a different room so that the nurses could keep a closer eye on me. It was my first meeting with the registrar, Paul McArdle. He was smiling as he informed me that Mr. Williams had been very pleased with what he had found. There was another pleasant doctor, called Annie, who explained things to us and was most helpful.

Once the results were back, I was given a date for the main operation which Mr. Williams was going to perform at St. Richard's, in Chichester. It was set for 21st December, just four days before Christmas, but we didn't mind because we didn't wish to lose any more time. Had we had to wait until after Christmas it would have coincided with the flu epidemic.

I arrived at St. Richard's during the evening, for my operation the following day. I was in Wittering Ward again but in a different bay. Roger and I chatted with the other patients who seemed friendly. I was making the most of still having a voice of some sort. It had begun to return but had become lower, hoarser and quieter than before.

During the operation, I had to have a tracheostomy fitted again so, once more, I was unable to speak. After the operation, I was wheeled into my own room in Intensive Care.

Once again, I had wires and tubes attaching me to various machines, which made all sorts of bleeps at intervals to alert the nurse on duty to perform the required action.

I distinctly remember Mr. Williams coming to visit me, afterwards, in ebullient mood. He told me that it had gone very well,

"We managed to do everything we wanted to do. Excellent! Excellent!"

He was beaming from ear to ear. It had evidently gone better than even he had anticipated. I knew people had been praying for me and also for him, during the operation, so I wasn't surprised at the outcome but, nonetheless, I was very pleased indeed.

I was disappointed that I had had to have another tracheostomy as the previous one had only just healed but I hoped it wouldn't have to be in for too long. Unfortunately, it meant yet more coughing and suctioning besides feeling very tender and sore after radiotherapy.

I didn't see my face for a few days but when I looked in the mirror, for the first time, I was horrified. It was extremely swollen, yet this was meant to be when it had improved. My tongue was enormous and could not be contained inside my mouth. My teeth rested on it, which made deep indentations all around it, both above and below. The doctors were afraid that I might bite through my tongue because of the pressure. It was to become almost unbearably sore over subsequent days. They could have given me a bung to spread the load but I had had my jaw cut in two on one side, to give access to my throat, and had had a titanium plate screwed into it. They didn't want a bung to alter the alignment of my jaw before it had reset.

Nerves had had to be severed, in my neck, so it was as though I had had a massive injection at the dentist's, except this didn't go away again. In fact, I was told that it could remain so indefinitely; it was like having a stroke and that I would have to wait for the nerves to regenerate. I would then have to learn to speak again.

23: 29TH JANUARY 2000

On 2nd January 2000, I was allowed home to recuperate, returning weekly or fortnightly to the hospital for consultations. All seemed to be going well until one Saturday at the end of January, a day we shall never forget. I had been on my own for an hour and a half while Roger had gone shopping. He had only just come inside, when I began to cough into a tissue, which I held up to my tracheostomy tube. I looked in astonishment at the tissue. I had coughed up a bright red patch of blood! Roger asked anxiously,

"Shall I ring the doctor, or should I dial 999?" I could not speak. We both stared as I coughed again, and blood spurted like a fountain. I had begun to haemorrhage through my tracheostomy tube at an alarming rate. Roger knew immediately what he had to do. He rang for an ambulance and was told it was eight to ten minutes away. He thought, 'We can't wait eight to ten minutes!'

I had been sitting at the kitchen table but had hurried over to the sink. The blood was gushing out in spurts, typical of arterial bleeding. It was also becoming thicker. There was nowhere that I could apply pressure to arrest the flow. I was suddenly aware that I could be about to die. I spoke to God,

'Oh no, I knew You'd healed me, but I didn't know that it would be for such a short time.'

I knew that if I were about to spend eternity with God, I wanted to be as right as possible with Him so I prayed for forgiveness for as many things as I could remember and forgave others although I had done this several times before. It was amazing because God was helping me by flashing pictures of people in front of me to remind me of people for whom to pray; He is so gracious.

I knew that Roger was greatly distressed, and I felt I hadn't said goodbye to our two sons properly; they were expecting me to get better and would be so shocked if I were to die without warning. Suddenly, I had a clear revelation,

'Hang on, I don't have to die. God created the Universe - the stars and the planets. He made us so it must be easy for Him to mend us.' I was remembering Colin Urquhart's book, which I had read in hospital. He had pointed me to the words in the Bible which say that

"Anything you ask in Jesus' name, believe it is yours and it will be done."

Nothing is impossible for Him. I pleaded with Him to spare my life,

'Please, please, please let me live. Please, please, please let me stay here longer and be a witness to Your glory.'

This was desperate; I repeated my plea earnestly, to make sure that He knew,

'Please, please, please let me stay here longer and be a witness to Your glory.'

I had read a book called "Beyond the Veil", which had been written by a young Muslim woman, who had converted to Christianity after Jesus had healed her when she had prayed to Him. She had asked God to use her as a witness, which led her to having amazing experiences. I wondered what I was letting myself in for, but I was willing to find out. I thought, I've done all I can. I am in God's hands. I've told Him what I want but it's up to Him. If He wants to take me to Heaven that's fine; if He keeps me here, that's fine. The outcome is up to Him. I felt perfectly at peace.

I was feeling tired and knew I could soon lose consciousness; therefore I would soon need to lie down so that my head would be as low as possible. This meant that blood would be able to reach my brain more easily and I would remain conscious for as long as possible. I was worried about the blood, which was still gushing out, making a mess on the floor for someone to clear up. Where should I lie? The utility room had ceramic tiles, which would be easy to wipe clean but was further away from the front door; the hall would be the nearest point of access for the paramedics, when they arrived, but the carpet would be ruined and more difficult to clean, so my best option was to remain in the kitchen as we had carpet tiles, which wouldn't ruin the whole floor and would involve spoiling only a few tiles, which could be washed. I lay down on the floor in the recovery position. It was amazing because, at the end of term, the school had provided a compulsory First Aid course. Little had I known how quickly I would be making use of this recently acquired knowledge.

Roger was speaking to the lady at the Emergency Services. The ambulance was still four to five minutes away and it was later estimated that I had lost four and a half pints of blood in five minutes. As I lay on the floor, the bleeding, which had been spurting out, slowed to a trickle and then completely stopped!

I noticed that the inner tracheostomy tube

had come out and was lying under the table, but I had no way of telling anyone that we needed to take it to the hospital. The lady at the Emergency Services had evidently just been explaining to Roger how to put me into the recovery position because I heard him saying,

"She's already done it!" in an incredulous voice. Both of them seemed amazed. God is so good; He knew that I would need to know this and had provided me with up-to-date information.

I was a dead weight when the ambulance crew lifted me onto a stretcher and took me out of the house. As they carried me from the kitchen, I was longing for someone to notice the silver tracheostomy tube lying on the floor, albeit under the table. Once inside the ambulance, they connected me to a saline drip and kept me conscious by asking me endless questions; I think I had to blink a certain number of times in reply.

On arrival at St. Richard's, I recognised certain members of the team. I'd seen Andrew Cronin, the registrar, only the day before. The anaesthetist was familiar, too. I was wearing some of my favourite clothes, including a brand-new French bra, so it wasn't much fun having them cut off but these things aren't important in the grand scheme of things. Making a sad yet comical face at the person with the scissors, I nodded in compliance. At this point I lost consciousness. Apparently, Mr. Williams had arrived and it was decided that I should be given a blood transfusion immediately and that I would be given an operation to discover the cause of the bleeding about ten days later, after it had settled down.

24: OH, NO, NOT AGAIN!

The events which took place on the evening of the 6th of February 2000, are etched on my memory and on the memory of all those involved.

There had been several visitors on the ward that day as it was a Sunday. Roger was with me and it was now evening. He had been showing me things of interest as usual.

Suddenly I coughed. A bright red patch of blood appeared on the tissue I held in front of me. Roger and I both looked at it in horror and our eyes met. Oh, no, not again! We both knew instantly what it meant.

Having a tracheostomy tube, to enable me to breathe, meant that several times, throughout the day and night, my throat would tickle which caused me to give an involuntary cough, frequently quite hard, thus permitting secretions from my lungs to be expelled via the opening in my throat. This had been one such occasion. However, in this instance, along with the normal secretions, was the unmistakable crimson of fresh blood.

My heart sank. This had happened eight days earlier, which is the reason why I had been readmitted to hospital, in an emergency, only a week before and was now awaiting an operation to find where the bleeding had originated.

I felt cheated. I had been trying so hard to get better, forcing myself to walk up and down the corridor linking the different bays with the aid of my drip stand. I had been advised that this activity would aid my recovery and help the post-operative swelling to go down more quickly but now, with a single cough, I was back to square one.

As I sat upright in bed, the familiar sight of the thick, bright red arterial blood began to gush out of my tracheostomy tube, splashing in a pool on to my white cotton nightdress and the hospital blanket. I tried to move my precious notepad aside.

Roger, who had seen it all before in our home the previous weekend, immediately rushed to the desk. Momentarily, it had been his first reaction to dial 999! He told the Sister on duty who put the emergency procedure into practice.

Two newly qualified doctors and a student doctor happened to be seeing a patient, on a routine visit, in the next bay. Initially, they saw no need to hurry as they couldn't imagine an MFU patient facing a life-threatening situation but, as soon as I came into their view, they were shocked and raced to my aid. The adrenaline was high. Although they had never witnessed anything like it before they worked fast and competently. I prayed hard that God would help the doctors know what to do; they seemed so young. The three worked superbly as a team, inserting lines into my arms and legs. Although I have a dislike of needles, in this sort of situation, the doctors could have done almost anything to me. I did not mind at all. My arms and legs were totally relaxed. I was like a rag doll. The will to survive takes over and everything else is subordinated.

Tim Kane, the young doctor with the glasses, had taken command and had called immediately for the anaesthetist. This turned out to be Dr. Guy Turner whom I recognised from a previous operation and whose arrival comforted me greatly. Even so, as the blood was surging relentlessly out of my tracheostomy tube, I had to take the opportunity, between surges, to breathe in through the same tube as this was the lifeline to my lungs. I must admit to having had a feeling of panic at this point because the bleeding was coming so fast that I thought I might not be able to breathe much longer. Unable to speak or to write anything down, as my arms and hands were too weak, I looked straight into the anaesthetist's eyes imploringly and then down to the tube and back again, trying my best to convey to him what was in my thoughts. He stood reassuringly at my head and I was so grateful for his calm presence. I am sure it must have given those young doctors reassurance too. I think my eyes must have closed for some of the time. I distinctly remember wishing that I could be asleep but having to be aware of what was happening to me.

Sarah, the nurse in charge that evening, appeared through the curtains at intervals to give me words of assurance. I appreciated her thoughtfulness. I remember opening my eyes at one point and seeing the familiar faces of Graham Smith, one of the registrars, who had come over from the Queen Alexandra Hospital in Portsmouth and Paul McArdle, one of the two senior registrars currently at St Richard's. Both wore serious expressions. I don't know how long they had been standing there. At that moment Mr. MacPherson, the surgeon, arrived. My relief was immense. I now knew all was well. My eyes did not leave him as he walked around my bed and came and put his hand comfortingly on my shoulder while he assessed the situation. I continued to pray that he would be guided to know what to do for the best.

I was still losing a lot of blood and they must have started a transfusion because I wondered why it was that they had this ready so quickly when previously I'd had to wait a few hours for cross-matching of blood. I remember watching my legs trembling uncontrollably, by this time, which reminded me of being in labour. I must have relaxed once Mr. MacPherson arrived. As he stood there, I wondered what was going on inside his head.

The team continued to work around my bedside. There was concern that the bleeding still gave no sign of abating. Decisions were being made. At one point I heard someone announcing,

"We're running out of blood!"

I do not recall much of what was being said during this time, but I remember clearly the bustle and excitement of leaving the ward and going to Theatre. A voice spoke with authority,

"Everything is ready."

I remember everyone making sure I had all the necessary drips and the bed being wheeled out of the bay, along the corridor, past my friend, Pat, and also, unknown to me, past Roger. I felt almost like an outside observer noticing that I was now more relaxed and that my breathing was steady, coming as it was between the spurts of blood. I began to feel uncomfortably cold as the cooler air of the corridor rushed past me. My blanket had been removed and I needed something warm to cover me. I was desperate to communicate this to someone but realised I had no means of doing so. We were moving in the direction of the Operating Theatre. Suddenly I knew no more.

25: RECOVERY

"Susan, Susan, wake up. Are you awake?" I don't remember the exact words, but I do recall the sensation of being aroused from a time of oblivion by the urgent voice of a nurse. I became conscious once more, yet it felt like a dream. I did not know where I was, who these people were or the time of day. What was happening? What was I doing here?

Everything seemed misty at first. I could move only my eyes at that point. There was no-one around. The person who had spoken these words seemed to have disappeared. I wondered why it was so important that I had had to be awake. What was the urgency? As I listened to the sounds around me and lay quietly observing my surroundings, I could see a nurse at the desk. She seemed to be fully occupied. Occasionally another member of staff would approach the desk and speak to her or use the telephone.

Curtains were drawn on either side of my bed, shielding me from other unseen patients nearby. I was aware that someone, perhaps a nurse or even a doctor, was seeing to the person on the other side of the curtain to my left. I had the distinct impression that the needs of these other patients seemed to be far more pressing than my own. I could not understand why no-one appeared to be taking any notice of me. Why had there been this compelling urge to wake me up for no apparent reason?

I continued to look around the room, trying to make sense of my world. All the lights were on. It must be evening. I needed to know the time. My eyes searched fervently for a clock. At last, I saw it - eleven o'clock. Oh, no, it must be almost midnight. I had missed visiting time. The disappointment was enormous. I always looked forward to seeing my visitors so much and I know my husband would have come to see me. Now I would have to wait until the next day.

A group of doctors suddenly came into view. They were dressed in loose blue cotton trousers and tops, white shoes and something resembling a J-cloth tied on their heads. They had appeared from my left and now proceeded to move across to the far side of the room, in a group. I watched them as they conversed with one another and moved around. They all went into a room off the large area where I was situated. Somehow I knew there was a man in there who was very ill. I could see, through the window of his room, that there were medical personnel with him. It must be serious. I wondered what had happened to him. Perhaps he had had a road accident.

Eventually the doctors emerged for another discussion. This was when they opened the door of the next room. Joy! I saw daylight through a window. The sky was clear and blue. It was a sunny day. It must be midday not midnight. I would see my visitors after all.

These are my reminiscences of that twilight time when I awoke after major surgery and a particularly long period of anaesthesia rendering me unconscious for about thirty-six hours. I was in Intensive Care. I had already been there twice before during the earlier part of my illness - after the first biopsy and other major surgery, yet I did not recognise it. To me, it was a foreign land.

26: THE TALK OF THE HOSPITAL!

The second haemorrhage had caused a stir; it was the talk of the hospital. Two of the nurses on duty on the ward that night were given prizes. Everyone was saying how traumatic it had been. I supposed it was because the bleeding wouldn't stop; I had been losing blood as fast as it was being put into me. After forty minutes to an hour, with doctors working around my bedside, I had been taken to Theatre for a three hour operation.

Roger had decided to wait at the hospital until the operation was over. The sister told him that she would keep him informed as soon as she heard anything. It must have seemed a long wait but he was praying for a good outcome and didn't want to go home without knowing how the operation had gone. At one o'clock or half past one Mr. MacPherson, himself, came to tell Roger the news:

"Well," he said, "She's all right.....The carotid artery and jugular vein had burst. I've tied off the lingual artery in the tongue, but I've decided to keep her sedated for thirty-six hours until the main operation, which will take place as planned." Roger thanked Mr. MacPherson for taking care of me and was free to go home with a grateful heart.

I later learned that an anaesthetist had had to sit at the foot of my bed for the whole of the following thirty-six hours, keeping me in a stable condition. Eventually, Mr. MacPherson told us that he hadn't warned us that this could happen because it was such a remote possibility and he hadn't wanted to worry us unnecessarily. I think he had made the right decision.

On the Tuesday, the previously planned operation went ahead with Mr. Williams as surgeon, which had been his intention. On reading his book, comprising two large tomes, which I'd had to order from the British Library, I learned that he advised other surgeons to wait for the immediate trauma to pass before operating, if at all possible, so that they could work in optimum conditions. This was to ensure the best possible outcome. It must have been a shock to him when I had haemorrhaged a second time but all had worked out well. The teamwork at St. Richard's was excellent.

I remember one of the registrars, Andrew Cronin, telling me that they had tied off the carotid artery and the jugular vein. He explained that they are like two pipes and it was like putting a stopcock on each of them, except that it wouldn't be reversed. I reacted with consternation. I'd always thought that these were very important blood vessels. Surely I needed both of these to carry the blood to my brain or other organs and back to the heart. Wouldn't I suffer brain damage or lose certain functions? Andrew assured me that I would be all right and that other blood vessels would compensate for this loss. There had been no alternative.

27: HIGH DEPENDENCY WARD

I had desperately wanted to live but after I left Intensive Care, I felt especially vulnerable. I felt tearful and I didn't feel at all well. I had a burning sensation in my throat. It was 4am but the nurse phoned the MFU doctor. I began to be sick. This continued in spite of two different types of anti-sickness injections.

I was huddled over a cardboard bowl, aware that my nightgown was in disarray and my back partly bare, when both consultant surgeons arrived with an enormous retinue of doctors and students. I felt absolutely terrible and didn't even have the energy to write so I was completely unable to communicate. The consultants both took the trouble to bend down and look me in the eye as they spoke to me. I appreciated their efforts. Inches from my face, Mr. MacPherson remarked,

"I'm right in the firing line here, aren't I? But I'm willing to take the risk! Poor old you, how do you feel? Does the sickness come in waves?"

I longed to tell him that he was in no danger at that moment and that the sickness didn't come in waves. I always knew when it was about to happen but was unable to give any warning to anyone. Soon it was Mr. Williams' turn,

"Are we feeling a little sicky? We'll see what we can do for you."

'A little sicky' was an understatement.

My mind was perfectly lucid. I wanted so much to be able to converse with them but there was nothing I could do. It was even worse than being at the dentist with one's mouth stuffed with cotton wool or other paraphernalia when the dentist asks a question which needs an answer. Mr. MacPherson was full of compassion, which I both needed and appreciated. Mr. Williams was very pleasant and fatherly. He said, "Progress is slow but it's progress." He was always positive.

I hadn't liked being moved from ITU (Intensive Care) to HDU (High Dependency). On Intensive Care, the ratio of patient to nurse is one to one and, not being able to communicate, I had been frightened that I might not be able to attract the nurse's attention quickly enough whenever she left my bedside. She told me she would be watching me but I still had a feeling of anxiety. I had been put on a ventilator as I was unable to breathe unaided.

"As soon as you are able to breathe on your own, we shall move you to the next ward," I was informed. The thought of having the ventilator switched off terrified me. It was a scary proposition. In fact, the procedure went smoothly. Taking deep breaths was hard work but the nurse who was with me was gentle and reassuring.

The Intensive Care nurses had all been extremely caring. The atmosphere must have been both hot and dry because one of the nurses was kind enough to rub some Vaseline onto my lips and cream on my face as I had nothing like that with me. Such kindnesses as this meant so much to me.

It was time for the transition to High Dependency. I was leaving everyone I knew; I felt very vulnerable. The door opened and I was wheeled through to my new surroundings. I looked for a clock on the wall so that I would know the time but it was nowhere to be seen. I felt lost. The patient/nurse ratio was 2:1. The nurse assigned to look after me introduced herself, but it was difficult to respond as I couldn't speak or write. Suddenly I couldn't cope.

I felt utterly depressed. I couldn't understand why I felt like this; it was so unlike me. When I had first been admitted to hospital, I was dismayed to find that the person in the next bed to mine kept on crying all the time. My initial reaction had been to think, 'Come on, pull yourself together.' Yet now, here I was being on the verge of tears almost all the time. The nurse did her best,

"Come on, Susan, is it something I've done? Shall I dance a little jig for you to cheer you up? Everybody tells me you're always so cheerful." She continued to try to humour me but it wasn't her fault. I was at a loss to know the reason why I felt this way.

After they had spoken to me, Mr. MacPherson and Mr. Williams conferred with each other. They decided to put my liquid feed into my stomach continuously so that it would push the blood, which had gone down into my stomach during the haemorrhage, out of the stomach as quickly as possible because that might be what was making me sick. The feed was therefore pumped in non-stop. My stomach began to become more and more bloated. I continued to feel and to be sick. I really appreciated it when the nurse took compassion on me and stopped the pump. Relief! I would now have some rest. This nurse had been obedient to the consultants' wishes but she was prepared to use common sense. She was sensitive to my needs. I had found a friend.

While I had been in Intensive Care, I hadn't realised how much any of the nurses had taken a real interest in me apart from a merely professional standpoint, so I was delighted when the last ITU nurse to have looked after me came through to HDU to see how I was. It was so kind of her. I had thought she would have been glad that I had moved on because she had had to do such a lot of unpleasant tasks for me. Even when one is extremely ill, there is still a question of dignity and it is very difficult being unable to perform certain tasks for oneself. One can feel quite sensitive and really sorry for the person having to do it.

The same applied here in HDU and later on, when I was on a different ward and I was asked if I would come back as a nurse once I was better, I gave a most emphatic, "No!" I had seen too much of the less pleasant side of caring for patients and it didn't appeal. I certainly admired the nurses for their care and devotion.

It was while I was in HDU that I felt at my lowest ebb. Later, when I asked about this, Andrew Cronin, one of the registrars, explained that my body had gone into shock through having the blood transfusions and from being under sedation for so long. It had been at this time that I had told my sister-in-law, Jennifer, that I couldn't take any more.

Jennifer prayed for me to forget the trauma; I was having dreams every day and night of the blood gushing out of my trache' tube.

During my time on the High Dependency Ward, a male nurse arrived called Simon. He was kind and even escorted me to visit Wittering Ward once I was strong enough. I was under the impression that I would soon be moving back there. I had really missed listening to the other women. How I longed to get back and see them all before the people I knew had gone home. My hopes were dashed when my nurse told me that when Mr. Williams had heard about my and others' expectations he said,

"No one is going anywhere unless I say so."

At the time I felt that he didn't understand but, in retrospect, I can see that he had my best interests at heart, wanting to make sure that I had recovered properly and was strong enough to cope with being on a main ward with a higher patient /nurse ratio. He may also have been trying to save the staff and patients there from the anxiety that my presence might have caused as they might possibly fear a repetition of that traumatic episode.

Eventually, it was time to move on to

Wittering Ward. The nurse helped me to prepare my things. She and I had developed a good relationship and I would miss her.

28: LEARNING TO SPEAK

Whilst I was still in High Dependency, the doctors were keen for me to start speaking again and had fitted me with a tracheostomy tube with a flap so that when I breathed out, the expelled air from my lungs passed through /over my vocal chords, thereby emitting sound through my mouth. Meaning well, the nurse encouraged me,

"Wouldn't it be nice if you gave the doctor a surprise and said 'Good morning' when he comes round?" Eager to do this I tried my best,

"uh….mor……ni," I tried again – the same result. It was no good. I quickly realised that some sounds were too difficult to say at present.

Paul Mc Ardle, one of the registrars, had said to me:

"Susan, because of what's happened to you, it will be like a baby or someone who has had a stroke. You are going to have to learn to speak all over again." I was shocked; would it really be like that? Would it take as long as that? Now I was beginning to find out. I decided to see which sounds I could make, hence going through the alphabet letter by letter. Like a child learning phonics, I tried to sound out each letter phonetically: "a" as in apple, "b" as in button, c for cat was too difficult; I could merely say, "t" instead of a hard c. Persevering, I continued to test out my ability to make a recognisable sound and noting down those letters. The next step was to see how many words it was possible to make using those letters. It was a challenge and the nurse had given me a target. I was determined to surprise the doctor. Compiling a list of possible words, I proceeded to make up a few short sentences.

"Hello, how are you?"

Andrew Cronin rose to the occasion,

"I'm very well, thank you. How are you?" To which I was able to say,

"I'm fine." That was it. My first sentences! What a sense of triumph!

The nurse who had encouraged me smiled.

The whole process of being unable to speak for several months has made me acutely aware of the frustration felt by anyone who finds themselves in such a situation. It must be particularly difficult for people who have had a stroke or for those with cerebral palsy or any illness which has affected the ability to speak and to write. There have been amazing advances in technology, which can help in certain cases. I often wonder what a person is thinking when their thoughts are trapped inside their head. When I was in that situation, too weak to write, my mind was racing. I had perfectly formed sentences in my head but no way of conveying them.

29: THE FOLLOWING YEAR

During that first year, I had regular consultations with my surgeon. One day Mr. MacPherson had to attend a course so, instead of seeing him as originally planned, I saw Mr. Williams and so it continued. I felt very sad at not seeing Mr. MacPherson any more but the main thing in Mr. Williams' favour, although he may not realise it, was that he never used an endoscope on me; he was now able to use a mirror and a torch, which was a wonderful relief. I liked Mr. MacPherson very much but he had said once that the nasendoscope would become my flexible friend over the coming years, which had filled me with dread. I was so glad I no longer had to endure that.

I missed Mr. MacPherson for a while, as he had had the most contact with me right from the beginning, but I soon became used to seeing Mr. Williams and, as he'd taken over my case and had performed the main operation on me in December 1999, he knew a lot about me. I could hardly speak during my earlier visits to him but I remember going one day and having quite a long conversation with Andrew Cronin, one of the registrars, who had always been so kind and understanding towards me. I was thrilled with my new ability to communicate without having to rely solely on pen and paper. The other registrar, Paul McArdle, had been the person who'd given me the most encouragement at the beginning of my struggle to speak again. He had such a wonderful sense of humour, which made it fun and took away the fear. It has been more difficult to learn to speak with a frozen tongue and after major surgery than it had been when my voice gradually came back after the drying out effect of radiotherapy.

Stephen Bloch, my speech therapist, was wonderful in his understanding of my problems and helping me to develop my speech as far as possible. I made the most rapid progress between February and July 2000. All along he had realised that any progress was impeded by the immobility of my tongue. In the October he felt frustrated saying that he wished he could take my tongue out, wring it and put it back in so that I could move it properly and be able to talk as I did before. I know exactly how he felt.

He gradually encouraged me to concentrate extra hard on certain sounds, particularly during the course of normal conversation, which has proved to be a marvellous way of improving my speech. Some people, particularly men, have found it difficult to understand me, especially at first, but women, on the whole, seem to concentrate more naturally on listening harder and making sense of it.

One of the biggest triumphs came when I was first able to speak over the telephone. For a long time it was and still can be the quickest and most effective way of dealing with nuisance phone calls.

At first, before I could make any sound, I used to tap the phone to let the person at the other end know that I was there and could hear them but it was frustrating not being able to speak. Gradually, I was able to make myself understood by speaking slowly and carefully. There are still sounds I cannot make very well and I collapse in laughter with the friend at the other end whilst I am attempting to find alternative words. It is like playing charades and can be hilarious. It has been an important step towards feeling less isolated.

It is still difficult to make myself understood

completely, especially when ordering prescriptions or giving my date of birth, for example, but Roger normally helps me.

Mr. Williams always had a positive attitude. One of the best pieces of advice he gave me very early on was,

"Do whatever you feel like doing and you will be able to do even more."

It is so true. His confidence and encouragement were very important to me, especially during those early days.

30: MEETING DR. TURNER, EARLY 2001

It wasn't until a year after my second haemorrhage that I was visiting St. Richard's, when whom should I meet coming towards me but Dr. Guy Turner, the anaesthetist who had been present during that traumatic event. What a wonderful surprise to see him again! He seemed delighted to see me, too, and told me that his wife had admired the watercolour I had painted and used for our Christmas card. I was pleased that he remembered it and that they had both liked it.

As we chatted, he suddenly amazed me by saying,

"Of course, if I hadn't come along when I did it would have been curtains for you."

I was stunned.

"What do you mean?" I asked.

"Well, the blood in your tracheostomy tube had become clogged and you'd stopped breathing; you had no pulse – your heart had stopped." This was astounding news! No-one had ever mentioned it to me before.

"What happened?" I enquired.

"I pushed a tube down inside and pumped oxygen into you as quickly as I could while I got Tim to suction away any blood."

"So, you saved my life!" I exclaimed, "Thank you, thank you, thank you." I had to give him an enormous hug of gratitude. A colleague of his passed by, at that moment, laughing and joked,

"Oh, they all think you're wonderful!" to which Dr. Turner replied,

"This is one of my star patients."

"He IS wonderful," I called out, "He has just told me that he saved my life."

When recollecting his thoughts of that evening, Roger had mentioned that one of the nurses had pressed a button and spoken out,

"Susan's crashed!"

Evidently, a grave emergency; no wonder two of the nurses on the ward that evening were given special prizes and the whole hospital had been abuzz with the story of this event. It had been more dramatic than I had, at first, realised.

God had certainly answered my prayer that the

doctors would know what to do. They had sent for the anaesthetist and Guy Turner had arrived just in time. Praise God!

31: FIRE BRIGADE CONFERENCE

For about two years after my operation I was not strong enough to go on holiday and one of the first trips away that we had was to attend the Fire Brigade Christian Conference in Scotland. These conferences were held annually, rotating between England, Scotland and Northern Ireland. Whilst attending the Conference in Scotland, Roger and I were having a chat with the Chairman, Ken Dyer, who was asking about my experience. Having listened to my story, he wondered if I would talk to everyone with Roger's help as my voice was still unclear and quite soft. I agreed.

That afternoon, Roger and I were in our hotel room where I was jotting down a few reminders in preparation for this and Roger was looking at the new Fire Fighters for Christ Bible we had been given. He opened it to look at it and it came open at Mark Chapter 5. His eyes alighted on verse 34, where he read, 'Jesus said to the woman, "You are now well because of your faith."' This seemed amazing that he should open it at that point when I was about to tell my story.

It wasn't until Roger recounted the incident to his colleagues at a Christian Fellowship meeting in the Fire Brigade offices, where he worked, that a friend asked,

"Was that the story of the woman with the issue of blood?"

On looking, we found that it was! As soon as she touched Jesus' garments, her bleeding stopped. This was further confirmation that, as Roger and I knew for sure, Jesus' hand had been at work in my healing. As I had reached out to Jesus in our kitchen, my bleeding, too, had stopped.

32: ST. ALBANS

About seven and a half years after my haemorrhage in the kitchen, Roger and I heard that Ken Gott was speaking at City Church in St. Albans in September 2007. Ken's father-in-law had run a church called Beth Shan in Newcastle-upon-Tyne, which we had visited as students there in the late sixties. I had recently read a book called 'The Sunderland Refreshing' concerning Ken's own church and we were keen to hear him, so we drove there for the day on Saturday, 22nd, September.

As well as Ken there was also another speaker that day, a prophetess who had the same name as an American actress, Sharon Stone. She asked certain people to stand up in turn while she prophesied to them. I had my eyes closed, listening, but Roger was looking, hoping she wouldn't come over to us. To our surprise, she came towards us, saying in a loud, commanding voice, "You two, stand up." We got up wondering what on earth was going to happen. Then, looking at me, she said, "The Sovereign Lord is telling me that He saved your life. Every cell in your body was closing down…….."

We were absolutely riveted. She was spot on. She'd never met us before and no one knew us. We had travelled quite a distance to get there. We listened intently to every word. It was a remarkable experience. After speaking to us, Sharon had a word for Ken Gott himself.

At the end, Sharon came across to speak to us together with Dave Campbell, whom we have subsequently met at River Camp run by Elim.

This had turned out to be a significant and blessed day, the most important being the message confirming God's saving grace. As Jesus says, "With men things are impossible but with God all things are possible."

33: REFLECTIONS

During my final week at Guildford, other women and I were put into a bay on the men's ward as there were more women oncology patients than men and because a mother and baby needed my room. The mother, who was feeding the baby herself, was admitted with breast cancer. My heart went out to her. There couldn't have been a better reason for having to give up my privacy, besides which I had started to feel somewhat lonely and missed the comradeship of others. I used to go and visit the friends I'd made in the main oncology ward I'd been in at first, but it isn't quite the same as being with them the whole time. There are advantages and disadvantages to both.

I had been sorry to be leaving my room but, on reflection, it was time for a change. The others in the ward were good company and, although I had to remain silent, I thoroughly enjoyed their jokes and repartee. There were serious times as well, but we supported one another and kept cheerful. This bonding with other patients is so helpful in the healing process. I have learned, through people I've met, that those with the most pain to hide tend to be the ones who are the life and soul of the party. There was one such lady in this ward. She had recently lost her husband, yet she made us laugh with her outrageous wit and made it her business to make everyone feel valued. We all loved her and missed her when she went home. One elderly lady was almost inconsolable.

In hospital, especially on an oncology ward as I was, one is surrounded by so many distressing cases that it puts one's own illness into perspective. I knew I had a long haul ahead of me but was confident that I would survive. I felt so sad when I heard the amazing stories people had to tell me. One of these patients told me that tumours had appeared in various parts of her body, one after another, and thus far had been successfully treated but the most recent one was in her heart. The doctors could no longer help her. She and her husband seemed so cheerful, but I could tell they were under stress. I hoped I could help by listening. I also prayed.

A few months later, I went to a concert where I met one of these ladies again. She was the mother of the young pianist who was performing that evening. She surprised me by saying that I had been an inspiration to everyone on the ward, with my smile and the way I'd coped. The irony is that they had all been an inspiration to me, in their various ways. Everyone has a different way of coping, and it helps to share experiences and support one another.

Once one has returned home, it is easy to become self-centred when, for months, people have been asking after one's own welfare. It is hard to remember, sometimes, that other people have their problems, too. Everyone does. Throughout my illness I have been shown great love and compassion and hope that I, in turn, can help others by being compassionate and more aware of their needs.

After months of staying indoors, apart from occasional short, slow walks in the winter and spring sunshine with my next-door neighbour, I was delighted when a friend, Elaine, asked me if I should like to go to an Art class with her. As she took me in her car, and I love painting and drawing it came at just the right time. I was still having to disappear to rinse my mouth quite frequently, but it didn't matter. It gave me something to look forward to each week. Elaine's next idea was to attend Creative Writing classes. At first, I didn't say anything, although it appealed, but when she told me that there might not be enough people to support the class, I said I'd come too. I thought that perhaps I should write a book after all. So many people had suggested it and I now felt that I was ready.

In those early days of my recuperation, it was a pleasure to potter about in the garden. My cousin, Jan, helped me with anything strenuous and she and a friend, Hazel, a former colleague of mine, took me to visit garden centres. Another source of enjoyment was that my husband and I resumed going to the concerts held by our local Music Society. At first, I had to sit by the door so that I could escape if I started coughing or needed to rinse my mouth, but I could eventually manage to wait until the Interval.

There has been so much to live for: simple things such as enjoying the sunshine and the beauty around us, listening to birdsong, spending time with family and friends, particularly my young grandson and new baby granddaughter. Most important of all was seeing the returning confidence of my husband and sons. Compared with a year before, we were making wonderful progress.

Another scare had made me aware, yet again, of the fragility of our existence and not to take it for granted. What the future held I did not know but I knew that I had been truly blessed. I have had a magnificent and dedicated medical team, caring family and friends and the prayer support of many people. I cannot yet speak properly or eat or drink, but I believe that, one day, all will be well. In the meantime, I am making the most of my life, a life for which I shall never cease to be thankful.

APPENDIX

Tell Your Story!

"Come forward if you want to know your destiny – your calling!" One of the African speakers at Faith Camp, an annual event organised by Colin Urquhart's church, was inviting us to come to the front and be prayed for. Many of us got up out of our seats and walked forward in response. I was still only halfway down the aisle when I heard God saying to me clearly, "Tell your story. Tell your story."

I have told people on an individual basis and in small groups but now, through the writing of this book, my hope is that it will reach more people so that they can hear about God's goodness and so that His name will be glorified.

It was after God saved me after my

haemorrhage that I told everyone about it. I could not keep quiet. I had to tell them whether by writing or speaking. He saved my life and has kept me here to tell it so I thank Him for what He has done and I hope that you will come to know Him for yourself if you don't already. I praise You, Lord Jesus!

Restoration

Writing a book about one's experiences is like unfolding the pages of one's life. When my story began, I was in a desperate state. I thought I was a Christian but, looking back, I know that my life was not honouring to God.

I remember saying to Christian friends, years ago, that I found it really difficult to submit my will to His. Basically, I wanted to live life wanting salvation whilst having my own way and making decisions for myself. When I made bad decisions, which inevitably happened, I used to tell God I was sorry, but I found I was doing this over and over again. It was not a satisfactory lifestyle.

Then, when I was dying at the kitchen sink, the Lord God Himself reached down from Heaven and rescued me. That is the simple truth. My life changed from that moment on. I have never been the same. I wish I had submitted my will to His sooner, but I am so glad He has allowed me to do it now. He is the God of second chances – He does heal and restore. He sent His Son, His only Son, Jesus to suffer and to die an agonising death on the cross to save us from our sins. He took our sins upon Himself so that we could be made clean by His blood. He has paid the price, the ultimate sacrifice, to make a way for us to come to the Father, our Father in Heaven, so that we could have a relationship with Him.

If you do not know Him, try reading the Gospels (good news), to be found at the beginning of the New Testament: Matthew, Mark, Luke and John, and even the Acts of the Apostles, who all but one, as far as we know, died horrible deaths for their faith. What was it that made them be prepared to die rather than renounce it? Think about it. Get to know Jesus for yourself – That is the reason He kept me here – to tell of His wonderful saving grace. He is always looking for the lost because He LOVES YOU so very much.

Printed in Great Britain
by Amazon

67695264R10090